WITHDRAWN FROM
KENT STATE UNIVERSITY LIBRARIES

A Service Profession,
a Service Commitment

A *Festschrift* in Honor of Charles D. Patterson

edited by
Connie Van Fleet and Danny P. Wallace

The Scarecrow Press, Inc.
Metuchen, N.J., & London
1992

Frontispiece: Photograph courtesy of Louisiana State University Office of Public Relations

British Library Cataloguing-in-Publication data available

Library of Congress Cataloging-in-Publication Data

A Service profession, a service commitment : a festschrift in honor of Charles D. Patterson / edited by Connie Van Fleet and Danny P. Wallace.
    p. cm.
  Includes bibliographical references and index.
  ISBN 0-8108-2640-2 (alk. paper)
  1. Library science--United States. I. Patterson, Charles D., 1928- . II. Van Fleet, Connie Jean, 1950- . III. Wallace, Danny P.
Z665.2.U6S47 1992
020'.973--dc20   92-39349

Copyright © 1992 by Connie Van Fleet and Danny P. Wallace
Manufactured in the United States of America
Printed on acid-free paper

CONTENTS

Preface i

Charles D. Patterson iv

Part I.   Roles in Support of the Professional Literature 1

    1.   An Editor Releases Energy
Kathleen de la Peña McCook 2

    2.   Reviewing: A Strategic Service
Dana Watson 19

    3.   Keepers of the Gates or Demons in a Jar?
John M. Budd 42

Part II.   Opportunities for Professional Action Through Organizations 70

    4.   ALISE and the Quest for Leadership
Danny P. Wallace 71

    5.   Beta Phi Mu: History and Future
Joseph Mika 104

    6.   The Institutional Service Role of the Librarian and Library and Information Science Educator in the Academic Setting
Bert R. Boyce 137

Part III. The Impact and Value of Teaching .. 154

    7. Advising and Mentoring: Complementary and Essential Roles
Connie Van Fleet 155

    8. Being a Damn Good Librarian
Donald E. Riggs 178

Bibliography 198

Publications of Charles D. Patterson 215

    Books, Chapters, and Articles 215

    Book Reviews (A Partial Listing) 220

Index 230

About the Contributors 247

PREFACE

"Never confuse fame with success. Madonna has one; Helen Keller has the other."[1]

Calling for leadership in library and information science has become a popular pastime and a recurrent theme. We speak of education for leadership, of recruiting leaders to the profession, and of developing untapped leadership potential. Leadership is of course vital, particularly as government and industry seem bent on a shortsighted path that will limit access to information, whether that path lies through legislation, regulation, judicial interpretation, or funding allocations.

We have not been very successful in defining professional leadership, often confusing a style that leads to public visibility with the substance that offers true vision for the profession. And along the way, we have overlooked the thousands of librarians who quietly and effectively bring about change through a lifetime of personal commitment.

Ours is a service profession; a great majority of librarians have developed a service ethic that is reflected in their daily interaction with patrons, and in the support that sustains our professional associations and literature. These individuals pay dues to professional organizations, serve on committees and boards, organize conference programs, and become faceless referees and unlauded reviewers. They guide new professionals through the formative first years of service and recruit others into the profession as they go about their daily work with enthusiasm, competence, and sensitivity. Most of all, they define librarianship in the minds of hundreds of thousands of patrons.

Charles Patterson is not an unsung hero; he has received a number of awards in recognition of his service to librarianship. Nor is he at work in the trenches; as a library and information science educator his direct contact with the public is limited. But his life reflects the service commitment of many dedicated librarians, even if it does not mirror it.

Just as librarians must have faith that each interaction, each effort, affects over time the nature and quality of the life of patrons, so educators must have faith that they will have an effect through their students. The impact is delayed, pervasive, and not immediately visible, but we must believe that it is genuine and important. This article of faith sustains many service professions; it is the lodestar of librarianship. This collection of essays, presented as Dr. Patterson steps down from a long and productive term as advisor for the Beta Zeta chapter of Beta Phi Mu and prepares for retirement from the professorial ranks, is a tribute not only to Dr. Patterson, but to all those who have embraced the service commitment and made it manifest.

The editors wish to acknowledge and applaud the work of Christine Sink (graduate assistant, Louisiana State University School of Library and Information Science), who came late to this project and handled the essential tedium of proofreading and reference checking with good

Preface

natured determination and new-found skill. Our contributors deserve special thanks for dedicating their royalties to the Beta Zeta Chapter of Beta Phi Mu.

NOTES

1. Erma Bombeck, quoted in "Quotable Quotes," *Reader's Digest* 140 (May 1992): 23.

CHARLES D. PATTERSON

It's difficult to write Dr. Patterson's biography without remembering the old Southern adage: a yankee is a person from the North who comes to visit; a damn yankee is one who comes to stay. Fortunately for those in the deep South in Louisiana, Charles Patterson stayed, bringing with him a commitment to librarianship, a scholarly approach, and a national perspective.

Charles D. Patterson was born August 8, 1928 in Wahpeton, North Dakota, the second son of Charles Irwin and Inez Fern (Slagg) Patterson. He attended public grammar and high schools in Ellendale, North Dakota, Mitchell, South Dakota and Bemidji, Minnesota, and was awarded the Bachelor of Science with majors in history, music and speech from Bemidji State University in 1950.

Dr. Patterson's brief experience as a music teacher in Fargo, North Dakota (September-November, 1950) was interrupted by his induction into the military. He served two years in Japan and Korea, where he was a supply sergeant in an infantry regiment and achieved the rank of Sergeant First Class. He was decorated with the Japanese Occupation Medal, the Korean Occupation Medal, the Combat Infantry Badge, and the Bronze Battle Star.

After the war, Patterson moved quickly through increasingly responsible positions in library service. Beginning as a junior reference librarian at the University of Minnesota (1954-55), he later became head librarian at

Bemidji (Minnesota) State University (1955-58), and was Director of Libraries and Assistant Professor at Glenville (West Virginia) State College (1958-1962). During this time, he also served as organist of the Trinity Methodist Church in Glenville (1958-62). Patterson was an assistant professor in the college of Arts and Sciences and chair of the Department of Library Science at West Virginia University (1962-1966). He was active in the West Virginia Library Association, where he was Chair of the College and University Library Section (1960-1961), Chair of the Indexing and Publications Committee (1962-1966), member of the Executive Board (1960-1961; 1964-66), and editor of *West Virginia Libraries* (1963-66), beginning a lifetime commitment to professional service. He still maintains ties with West Virginia, which is a member of the Academic Common Market, and recruits students to Louisiana State University through publications and personal contact. He received the West Virginia Library Association Certificate of Appreciation in 1981.

Despite the demands of full-time employment and increasing professional responsibilities, Dr. Patterson continued to expand his educational preparation, receiving the Master of Arts (1956) with majors in library science, music, and education from the University of Minnesota, and the Master of Music (1964) with majors in organ and church music from West Virginia University.

Following his own advice ("Get your degree in the North if you want to live in the South."), Patterson moved to the University of Pittsburgh in 1966, where he was the recipient of the Faculty Scholarship (1966-1971) and was awarded the Advanced Certificate in Library Science (1968) and the Doctor of Philosophy in Library Science (1971). He was an instructor in the University of Pittsburgh School of Library and Information Science from

1966 to 1971, and an assistant professor from 1971 to 1972, during which time he served as program chair of the College and University Library Section, Southwest Chapter of the Pennsylvania Library Association (1971-1972). He was also President of the Tri-State Chapter of the Association of College and Research Libraries (1972-1973). He maintained his interest in music, serving as organist/director of the Third Presbyterian Church in Uniontown, Pennsylvania. In 1972, Patterson moved to Louisiana State University to become an associate professor in the Graduate School of Library Science (1972-1978). He was promoted to the rank of professor with tenure as a member of the graduate faculty in 1978.

In the subsequent two decades, Charles Patterson became involved in numerous activities in service to the school, the university, the community, and the profession. His work has addressed such topics as bibliographic instruction, editorial accountability, library education, and factors that affect effective reference service, and has appeared in a number of publications, including *The Video Annual*, the *Journal of Education for Library and Information Science*, the *Reference Librarian*, *Reference Services Review*, *RQ*, the *Bowker Annual*, the *ALA Yearbook*, the *Dictionary of American Biography* and *West Virginia Libraries*. (For a complete bibliography of Dr. Patterson's work, please see pages 215-220.) He is the author of "Origins of Systematic Serials Control: Remembering Carolyn Ulrich," which is considered the definitive work on this important figure. Patterson, editor of *Reference Services Review*'s "Landmarks of Reference" column since 1986 and consulting editor for Libraries Unlimited (1984-), is probably best known for his analyses of reference materials. He has written over one hundred reviews that have appeared in such diverse publications as

Charles D. Patterson

Research Strategies, *Journal of the American Society for Information Science*, *Information Processing and Management*, *American Reference Books Annual*, *Booklist*, and the *Journal of Library History*. (For a partial listing of Dr. Patterson's reviews, please see pages 220-229.)

A sterling example of his own philosophy in action ("Publish, party, and participate."), Charles Patterson has assumed service responsibilities at all levels. He began his career at Louisiana State University School of Library and Information Science as chair of the Curriculum Committee (1972-1977) and a member of the Library School Library Development Committee (1972-). He has also chaired the school's Policy Committee (1975-1979, 1987-), the Promotion and Tenure Committee (1983-1986), and the Academic Personnel Committee (1989-). The faculty is probably most grateful for Dr. Patterson's yeoman service as chair of the Steering Committee for the Committee on Accreditation Self-Study Report for three visits (1973, 1979, and 1984). In addition, he has served as faculty advisor to the Beta Zeta Chapter of Beta Phi Mu since 1974. The chapter is one of the most active in the United States due, in large measure, to Dr. Patterson's tireless attention to detail and innovations, including *Beta Zetings* (the chapter's newsletter) and an annual initiation banquet featuring national and international speakers. A member of Beta Phi Mu since 1971, he has served as chair (1983) and member (1982) of Beta Phi Mu's National Awards Jury and National Director-at-Large (1982-1985). Dr. Patterson received the American Library Association Beta Phi Mu Award "for distinguished service to education for librarianship" in 1989. The citation for the Award reads, in part,

> Professor Patterson served as a teacher and
> mentor of many students in the library

education program of Louisiana State University. He is a concerned, intelligent human being who has always given first priority to active professional service to librarians and libraries through the American Library Association, the Association for Library and Information Science Education, and Beta Phi Mu.

Patterson is well-known throughout Louisiana State University for his work at the university level. Bringing together his knowledge and love of librarianship and music, he has served on the university's Faculty Senate (1972-1977), the Archive and Records Management Committee (1976-1979), and the Performing Arts Committee (1979-1982). He has been a member of the University Chamber Music Society since 1976, serving as president (1978-1980) and treasurer (1980-), and of the American Guild of Organists, serving as Dean (1985-1986), Sub-Dean (Baton Rouge chapter, 1984-1985) and Historian (1976-). A member of the American Association of University Professors since 1964, he has been Chair of Committee "W" (1975-1976), Secretary of the LSU chapter (1982-1983 and 1987-1988), and President of the LSU chapter (1985-1986). In 1984, Dr. Patterson was the recipient of the prestigious LSU Foundation H. M. "Hub" Cotton Faculty Excellence Award for "excellence in teaching, research, administration, and public service."

Active in state affairs, Dr. Patterson has served as a delegate of the Louisiana's Governor's Conference on Library and Information Services (1978) and been a member of several Louisiana Library Association committees, including the College and University Library Section Program Committee (Chair, 1973), the Continuing Education Committee,(1973-1975), the Scholarship Committee (1983-1986), and the Federal Relations Committee (1984-1988).

Dr. Patterson's service continues on the national level, as he currently serves on two American Library Association, Reference and Adult Services Division committees: Standards and Guidelines (1989-) and Research and Statistics (1990-). He also has been chair of ALA's Scholarship Committee (1972-1973) and a member of the Reference and Subscription Books Review Committee (1975-1977) and the RASD Professional Development Committee (1985-1989).

It is apparent that, as active as he has been in a number of associations, Patterson's top priority is education for librarianship. Beginning in 1973 when he served as chair for the Association of American Library Schools (AALS) Interest Group on Continuing Education, he has been an influential voice in matters of concern to library and information science educators. He has devoted eighteen years to fostering the exchange of ideas and research among members of the profession through his work on the *Journal of Education for Library and Information Science (JELIS)* (editor, 1984-1988), formerly the *Journal of Education for Librarianship* (editor, 1980-84, member of the editorial board, 1975-79). His contribution was recognized in 1988, when he was the recipient of citations of appreciation from the Board of Directors of the Association for Library and Information Science Education (ALISE) and from the Editorial Board of *JELIS*. Patterson continues to serve, most recently as Chair of the ALISE Awards Committee and Chair of the ALISE Retirees Interest Group.

Charles Patterson continues to make a genuine and deep impact in ways that are not documented in curricula vitae or listings from the *Social Sciences Citation Index*. As with most educators, his primary effect is at once the most important and most difficult to measure. During his years as a library and information science educator, Dr. Patterson has influenced scores of librarians with his knowledge, commitment, and sheer enthusiasm for our profession. And those librarians have influenced countless others, both patrons and peers. Perhaps Dr. Patterson continues to be an excellent educator, because he has never lost touch with his primary goal for himself and for his students -- "to be a damn good librarian."

Part I:
Roles in Support of the Professional Literature

*O*ne of the key characteristics of a profession is the existence of a meaningful body of scholarship reflective of the profession and its interests. Professional educators contribute to the literature in several ways, the most obvious of which is by acting as authors. The dedicated professional may also assume further responsibilities by acting as an editor, by becoming active in the support of book reviewing, and by acting as a peer reviewer for refereed scholarly and professional journals. Dr. Patterson has been notable for his activities in all three areas, having served as editor for the *Journal of Education for Library and Information Science*, contributed significantly to the reviewing of reference works, and having served as a frequent referee for a variety of publications.

In Chapter 1, Kathleen de la Peña McCook, a past editor of *RQ* and *Public Libraries*, discusses the roles and responsibilities of the editor of a scholarly journal. Dana Watson explores the nature of the service provided by the book reviewer in Chapter 2. Chapter 3, by John M. Budd, explores the benefits and problems of the refereeing process.

Chapter 1

AN EDITOR RELEASES ENERGY

Kathleen de la Peña McCook

*E*ditors, like librarians, are intermediaries. However, the direction of the mediation is a mirror-image. Librarians stand between the world of knowledge and the needer of knowledge, isolating and refining from huge amounts of data the particulars required to supply specific need. Editors stand between the specific person, the author, and the larger world that the author will address. Thus discussions of editing in library and information science present a set of issues unique for editors.

Editors of library and information science literature -- in most cases librarians first -- have lived out mediation from the universal to the specific. They then take this experience, do a 180 degree turn, and live out mediation from the specific to the universal. This mazurka is a lively dance, indeed. But, as the great Max Perkins -- the editor of all editors, the patron saint of the blue pencil -- once observed, "an editor releases energy."[1]

This essay first addresses the role of editors in general and second the role of editors in the library and information science disciplines. Its purpose is to demonstrate that editing, like librarianship, when performed with high standards of ethics, commitment, and ideals is one of those unsung labors that contribute to the world of learning in a steady and inexorable flow.

EDITING AS AN ACT

In her excellent essay, "Revise & Consent: The Author-Editor Relationship," Pedolsky points out, "As much as writing a manuscript is a creative, intellectual process for the author, so is editing a manuscript for the editor."[2] While the ideal of Max Perkins hovers about the psyche of all editors as a muse, the reality is that most editors are not honing the prose of the Great American Novelists. Most editors are working in technical fields for somewhat definable audiences.

The End is the Beginning (Identifying Audience)
Audience is all. For most editors the midnight dream of taking a work that is "good" for the world and making the world see that it is good is simply a dream. After all, editors do work for publishers and publishers want to sell their books or journals to pay the rent, pay their staffs and bring home a profit. So, somewhere between sublimity and lucre an audience must be defined and imagined.

This is hard and it presents a problem of elitism and hubris that all editors must face. Editors may begin their careers just like librarians begin their careers with an unrealistic sense of purpose. But, just as no library will fill its role if shelves are stocked only with unscannable poetry, no publisher will generate a balanced budget if catalogs are stocked only with ineffable prose.

Is the item to be edited for everyone in the world? Outside of the *Bible*, the *Qua'an*, the *Torah*, the *Pali Canon* or the *Bhagavad Gita* universal audiences are unlikely to be found. If the audience is a professional or technical one -- as is the case for those editing in library and information science -- the field is more easily defined but then refinements need to be factored into audience definition. Is it for all information workers? Is it for students? Is it for those in a specific library or information center type? Is it for scholars of the field?

Journal editors face the toughest challenge. Books have clearly defined market niches, but journals, over the long haul, for survival and viability need to appeal to a broader audience and need to sustain a tone and quality over time to ensure renewal of subscriptions. There is even a measurement of the impact and importance of journals through the *Social Sciences Citation Index* or *Science Citation Index* databases that can provide a rough indicator of influence and the scope of audience reached through citation analysis.

A good editor imagines the audience and inhabits the audience's world view as it shifts through the spirit of the times. The capacity to internalize the audience characterizes a good editor. Think of journals that have shifted in scope and tone over time . . . *Rolling Stone*, for example, has remained a viable publication as its initial audience aged, grew affluent and altered their values. *The Saturday Review*, as another example, failed miserably in its attempts to reorient to an imagined audience.

Sifting and Winnowing (Selecting)

Once the audience is clearly in mind with due respect to changes in demographics and subtle shifts of values and orientations, it is time to throw out the net and invite submissions. Editors that publish "instructions to authors" and wait for submissions to arrive will have varied experiences depending on the scope and base of the magazine's readership. Small special interest magazines may have difficulty in filling issues while large, broad-based publications may receive overwhelming submissions. However, even those editors fortunate enough to have a surfeit of material need to "work the crowd" to ensure a steady flow of quality material. This may be perilous. Authors urged to submit may produce work of poor quality. If refereeing is a requisite those urged may be rejected. A politic manner is required to increase submissions. The editor must know the difference between a good speech presenter and a quality writer. The times that a bevy of listeners run up to the podium and urge the speaker to submit the talk for publication, only to have a miserably shallow pastiche be submitted, are far more numerous than the times that a quality paper results.

It is best to have a buffer between the author and the editor. Judicious use of an editorial board or refereeing policy can prevent the "old buddy" system from taking hold; can refine average manuscripts to excellent; and can assist new authors. The romantic image of the lone-ranger editor cannot be sustained in a world as complex and geographically far-flung as today's.

The Final Word (Preparation for Publication)

Once a manuscript is accepted for publication, regardless of how it was selected, it is time for that final solitary evaluation of the editor and the manuscript. If sexist language must be omitted due to editorial policy, this must be done and the author's feelings soothed (this problem is disappearing, however, as most authors are no longer wedded to the male pronoun). Roughness of grammar and lexicon -- small matters indeed if the content is solid -- should be organized in conformity with the journal's style sheets.

If the magazine at hand does not submit galleys to authors and the lag between final acceptance and publication is going to be a long one it is important to communicate this to the author. Some authors need to know when their submission will be published for job-related reasons (tenure). For others it may be but a simple courtesy, but the editor should remember that the long hiatus between acceptance and publication is unnerving to old hands and often devastating to new authors.

These simple three stages in the editorial process iterated, let us now turn to the particular field of library and information science to see how these general principles apply.

EDITORS IN LIBRARY AND INFORMATION SCIENCE

With a characteristic lack of solidarity, librarians are prone to disparage their own literature. Art Plotnik has discussed this phenomenon noting, "a review of library literature tells us that most library writing is, well, abysmal" and goes on to observe, "the least appetizing writing habit of librarians is to snipe at everything in the profession, including its literature."[3] However, there is, at long last, a growing appreciation for the research base in the field. In a memo to American Library Association units soliciting opinions on a draft statement on "Education for Library and Information Studies in U.S. Universities," Standing Committee on Library Education (SCOLE) chair, F. William Summers wrote,

> The statement is designed to provide information and background on the role of schools of library and information studies in

U. S. universities, the nature of the field as an academic discipline and its important characteristics.[4]

In the section of the draft titled, "Research Base," it is noted:

> The development of a research base in library and information studies is a relatively recent occurrence. The field is in an evolving state and does not yet exhibit the maturity shown by disciplines that made the transition from practice to theory at an earlier time. Thus, one finds, for example, a greater utilization of exploratory and descriptive research design than might be the case in allied social science disciplines.[5]

Given this "evolving state," the role of the editor in library and information science is especially crucial. It is a role that has seldom been examined, certainly seldom appreciated. However, it is a role that holds the key to fostering development of the literature of the field to higher standards of rigor and excellence. The three primary components of editing -- identifying audience, selecting, and preparation for publication -- examined in the context of the disciplines of library and information science illuminate the importance of the editorial function.

Identifying Audience

As noted in the general discussion of audience, a good editor inhabits the audience's world view. However, the audience must first be defined. General interest periodicals such as *Library Journal* or *Wilson Library Bulletin* aspire to cover all the bases in a readable, lively and appealing style. The audience is broadly conceived. The success of these journals may well be measured by the scope of advertising in their pages -- a highly predictive indicator of perceived success at reaching an audience.

Advertising, in fact, is an aspect of journal editing that has not often been addressed in relationship to library and information science journals. Some, such as *Library Quarterly* or the *Journal of Education for Library and Information Science*, do not accept advertisements. Others, such as those published by the American Library Association (*RQ*, *Public Libraries*, etc.) actively seek it. For those journals actively seeking advertising revenue the need to "sell" potential advertisers on the merits of placing copy has often resulted in an analysis of readership which, in turn, assists editors in audience definition.

From time to time editorial boards attempting to align content with advertising needs have polled readers as to their preferences. For the most part, however, these polls have focused on current subscribers rather than potential readers. Thus the hard data available to editors in determining audience definition have either been gathered for expanding the advertising base or by querying those already receiving the publication. In the case of journals tied to membership in an association, the targeting of audience is closely allied to membership development.

Beyond these considerations, which give some indicators of audience, editors might gain additional insights by reviewing subscription lists, holding forums at professional conferences or visiting with librarians at their place of work.

An excellent example of audience analysis was developed by Charles D. Patterson in his "An Assessment of the Status of the Journal," in which he provided data on reader preference.[6] Such studies, often done internally by editors or editorial boards but not published, provide benchmark information on library and information science publishing.

Another dimension of audience identification comes from the value accorded the journal by external evaluators. These include studies such as those conducted by John M. Budd in his "Literature of Academic Libraries: An Analysis," in which he uses citation analysis to examine what journals can be identified as having articles relevant to academic librarianship and what specific titles are most frequently cited.[7]

Selecting

This author's experience with a number of library and information science journals has given insight into the amount of material "out there."[8] There is not a great deal. Submission rates do not approach the situation in the humanities and social sciences in which competition is fierce and backlogs extend to years. Quality articles in library and information science can always find a publishing outlet in less than two years -- an ideal situation for authors, but a difficult one for editors.

However, although there is not surfeit of articles, standards of rigorous review and refereeing have begun to be applied. The most recent assessment of the process of submission and selection among journals in library and information science is Budd's 1988 article, "Publication in Library and Information Science: The State of the Literature."[9] Budd found an acceptance rate of unsolicited manuscripts overall to be from 30.5% to 39.4%. He also noted that the submission rate seemed to be dropping in terms of manuscript submission compared to rising number of journals.[10]

Implementation of formal refereeing has accelerated in library and information science. Formal refereeing for this article means use of referees who are not members of the editorial staff or board. While peer review may be loosely defined to include these groups the level of rigor increases as opinions solicited increase in independence. Budd's study characterized six levels of evolution: "level 1" -- "editor alone decides" on up to the most rigorous "level 6" -- "referees who do not know the author's name decide."[11] Journals falling into "level 6" include *Library and Information Science Research*, *Library Quarterly*, and *RQ*. Budd found that between the period 1978 to 1988 the number of journals employing referees increased from six to twenty.[12]

The move to formal refereeing has not been an easy one. While journals affiliated with academic libraries were able to accommodate rigorous review in line with the norms of the university, others found the move more difficult. In the last editorial written as *RQ* editor this author observed:

> The benefits of refereeing are many. *First*, the quality of articles is enhanced through the evaluation process. *Second*, the journal gains scholarly credibility . . . *Third*, the communication among scholars is enhanced. . . *Finally*, the journal increases its impact on the field through dissemination of high-quality articles that are in turn cited and become the base for building new knowledge.[13]

This commitment to the refereeing process was carried forward to *Public Libraries*. When this author assumed editorship, *Public Libraries'* articles were largely solicited (Budd found in 1988 that only 20% came unsolicited compared to *RQ*'s 86%).[14] The selection process was completely in the hands of the editor. Movement from this "level 1" selection arrangement (editor alone) to "level 6" (referees who do not know the author's name decide/ double-blind) required numerous discussions with the editorial board and analysis of the norms of the field.

For the most part this process worked well. The process lengthened the time from "submission to publication" as manuscripts underwent extensive evaluation and revision. The change of policy for *Public Libraries* was reviewed by this author in a final editorial: "Behind each 'completed' manuscript lies a file of correspondence, referee comments and editorial suggestions."[15] However, before an evaluation could be made of the impact of moving *Public Libraries* from "level one" to "level six," a conflict between the editorial board and the editor resulted in a change of editor. If any observations might be made on the process of selection given my experience with two very different journals and editorial boards, it is that different audiences and different leadership perceive the role of journals from diverse perspectives. *RQ*'s editorial board had largely moved toward academic and scholarly norms with the emphasis on objectivity and impartiality that refereeing ensures. The *Public Libraries* editorial board had not had time to deliberate the rather abrupt change in policy vis-a-vis manuscript selection under my editorship that a shift from "level one" to "level six" effected. In retrospect it might have been better to have made the shift more gradually.

These tensions and discussions have certainly enriched the field, expanded the number of individuals analyzing the role and impact of journals and generally enhanced the understanding of scholarly communication. Clearly the "selection" responsibility of an editor in the library and information science disciplines indicates that the editor can be an active participant in the field's maturation.

The process of refereeing challenges an editor and requires a great deal of skill. The external, anonymous referees must be apprised of standards and worked with -- usually one-on-one -- to enable them to provide evaluations that are constructive. Even a full-blown "level six" evaluation configuration has a great deal of fluidity.

Taking *RQ* as an example, let us see how this works. An article arrives. The editor reviews referee profiles to decide to whom it ought to be sent for evaluation. (Referee profiles must be updated continuously). Referees receive an evaluation form but have ample latitude to make margin comments and general observations. If all goes well the evaluations are returned in a few weeks.

At this point the editor's skills are called upon. If the manuscript is rejected by both referees a lengthy letter from the editor may be required to provide constructive criticism. If the manuscript is accepted but subject to revision the nature of the revision must be made clear to the author in a letter from the editor. This process, in fact, is the heart of scholarly communication that strengthen's the field's research base.[16] The behind-the-scenes judgments and communications result in accepted manuscripts that have had the evaluation and counsel of at least three experts. Then and only than can a manuscript advance to the final editing stage.

Editing

By now it is clear that the actual "editing" -- sitting down with the author's final version of a manuscript and readying it for publication -- is but the final step in a series of activities that comprise the role of editor. There have been a number of fine articles that outline specific considerations for editing in library and information science. These include Alley and Cargill's "Editing Newsletters and Periodicals" [17] as well as Johnson's "The Journal Article" (from the author's viewpoint).[18]

The core skills of an editor need to meld with the particular requirements of the journal at hand. If the journal requires a prosaic bland style or a lively breezy style this needs to be factored into the final manuscript version. Essentially, a good editor has an instinctual gift for accommodating the two forces that drive the work -- the needs of the journal and the needs of the author.

MANAGING THE JOURNAL

This essay has focused closely on the journal article and the role of the editor in facilitating publication of articles through identification of audience and selection. However, the role of editor has many other facets. These other facets do not intrigue me as they are outside the intimate interaction that centers on the thoughtful written world. But, they do bear mentioning.

Skillful interaction with the editorial or advisory boards that oversee a journal is a requisite for successful management of a journal. This author has had extremely varied experiences along these lines.[19] Once understanding is established, editorial policies need to be forged and codified. These include matters of scope, style, advertising policy, reviewing policy and the like.

It is most helpful, too, if very standardized procedures are defined that govern acknowledgement of authors, communications to referees, deadlines and general oversight. A good example of the process of standardization of these sort of procedures may be reviewed in "*Public Libraries*: The Redesign, Reorganization, and Development from a Quarterly to a Bimonthly Publication."[20]

If journals include ongoing columns a great deal of work needs to be done with column editors to ensure consistency of format, standardization of style, and quality of material. Columns can provide coverage of important and crucial issues of concern to the audience that are not covered by unsolicited submissions. However, the proper balance between articles and columns will differ vastly from journal to journal. Monitoring audience reaction to columns is vital to the success of a publication. Generally, some sort of percentage should be assigned to columns and some percentage set aside for general articles. In reviewing issues I have edited of *Public Libraries* and *RQ*, those issues in which an overbalance of columns filled the pages generally resulted in a less than satisfactory issue.

Making sure that copy is sent in a timely fashion to the publisher with carefully labeled photographs, graphics, and lists of contributors who are to receive issues (or whatever compensation has been established) requires strong planning skills and a tenacity for deadlines. The editor, in turn, must exercise firm oversight on deadlines that feed into the final deadline. A given issue of *Public Libraries* or *RQ* involved the coordination of over fifty individual efforts to create the final submitted manuscript. Early identification of perennial late columnists or referees is essential if the entire effort is to flow as it needs to flow to publication deadline.

In addition to the steady and logical preparation of the final manuscript, editors assume all sorts of additional and unexpected responsibilities. These include calls from advertisers, complaints from injured authors of books reviewed, press releases, invitations to speak on the art of editing, the need to cover conferences, strong stands on acceptance of unsolicited manuscripts that someone on the board thinks must be published, and communications with would-be authors.

Taken together the demands on the editor to manage a journal combined with the work to edit a journal is a challenging task. The final result -- a completed issue -- reflects only a small portion of the effort required to produce it.

CONCLUSION

These reflections on editing are included in this volume because Charles D. Patterson was an indomitable editor for the *Journal of Education for Library and Information Science*. His reflections on editing, recorded in "Editorial Accountability: Ethics and Commitment," are essential reading for editors or those who would edit.[21]

In library and information science editing is largely an uncompensated activity. Even those editorships that pay a modest honorarium do not reflect the time put in. Why, then, do individuals step forth and undertake these tasks? In the cases of all editors with whom I have talked the motivating factors have been intrinsic satisfaction in seeing ideas shared, the ideals of the field explored and refined, and a belief in the work that librarians do. Development of a strong literature facilitates advancement of the profession and a service ethos.

NOTES

1. A. Scott Berg, *Max Perkins: Editor of Genius* (New York: E. P. Dutton, 1978), 6.

2. Andrea Pedolsky, "Revise and Consent: The Author-Editor Relationship," in *Librarian/Author: A Practical Guide to How to Get Published*, ed. Betty-Carol Sellen (New York: Neal-Schuman, 1985), 51.

3. Art Plotnik, "Secrets of Writing for the Professional Literature of Librarianship Without Losing Your Self-Esteem," in *Librarian/Author: A Practical Guide on How to Get Published*, ed. Betty-Carol Sellen (New York: Neal-Schuman, 1985), 79.

4. American Library Association, Standing Committee on Library Education, "Education for Library and Information Studies in U.S. Universities," draft distributed May, 1991, cover memo from F. William Summers, Chair.

5. Ibid., 3.

6. Charles D. Patterson, "An Assessment of the Status of the Journal," *Journal of Education for Library and Information Science* 25 (Spring 1985): 301-312.

7. John M. Budd, "The Literature of Academic Libraries: An Analysis," *College and Research Libraries* 52 (May 1991): 290-295.

8. Editor of *RQ*, editor of *Public Libraries*; editorial board of *Library Trends* and *Library Quarterly*: referee for the *Journal of the American Society for Information Science*, the *Journal of Education for Library and Information Science*; column editor for *Serials Review* and the *IASSIST Quarterly*; editor for state association newsletters.

9. John M. Budd, "Publication in Library and Information Science: The State of the Literature," *Library Journal* 113 (September 1, 1988): 125-131.

10. Ibid., 126-127.

11. Ibid., 128.

12. Ibid., 127.

13. Kathleen M. Heim, "Refereeing, Scholarly Communication, and the Service Ethos," *RQ* 27. (Summer 1988): 463.

14. Budd, "Publication," 129.

15. Kathleen M. Heim, "Editorial," *Public Libraries* 29 (November/December 1990): 327.

16. Heim, "Refereeing," 463-464.

17. Brian Alley and Jennifer Cargill, "Editing Newsletters and Periodicals," chap. in *Librarian in Search of Publisher: How to Get Published* (Phoenix: Oryx Press, 1986), 111-121.

18. Richard D. Johnson, "The Journal Article" in *Librarian/Author: A Practical Guide to How to Get Published*, ed. Betty-Carol Sellen (New York: Neal-Schuman, 1985), 21-35.

19. "ALA Division Editors: Censored or Edited?" *Library Journal* 115 (March 1, 1990): 54-55.

20. Kathleen M. Heim, "*Public Libraries*: The Redesign, Reorganization, and Development from a Quarterly to a Bimonthly Publication, June 1988-December 1989," report submitted to The Public Library Association (Baton Rouge: Louisiana State University, School of Library and Information Science, Research Center Annex, December, 1989).

21. Charles D. Patterson, "Editorial Accountability: Ethics and Commitment," *Journal of Education for Library and Information Science* 28 (Fall 1987): 83-86.

Chapter 2

REVIEWING: A STRATEGIC SERVICE

Dana Watson

*I*n the profession of library and information science, which is dedicated to the provision and dissemination of information, communication between members depends to a large extent on professional organizations and professional publications. Support of these organizations and their journals comes not only from subscription and membership fees but also to a certain extent from the volunteer time and effort supplied by members and their institutions. One volunteer service that members regularly perform is evaluating newly produced materials through the medium of published reviews. Although this is a process which takes time and skill and calls upon varying depths of expertise and experience, the rewards are largely intrinsic and the acknowledgement is scant. Librarians need the reviews and the assurance that materials will be evaluated, and evaluated fairly. Staff reviewers employed directly by professional journals cannot cover the entire range of today's publications; volunteer reviewers can serve the profession by dedicating some of their time and energy to ensure that reviews are available, that their quality is high, and that they reflect the needs of their colleagues. This cooperative though low profile effort can be mutually beneficial.

Deeper appreciation of volunteer reviewers, and perhaps in time better acknowledgement of the service they perform, can come through an understanding of the reviewing process. Knowledge of how reviews are utilized, of the review policies of particular journals, and about the indexing of reviews can shed light on this process. Information about the relative coverage by reviews of the titles published in a year, the ways in which reviewers benefit from writing reviews and about the characteristics and performance of volunteer reviewers can add to the picture. Also important are the essential components of reviews, and the role of the editor. Together these all contribute to a better comprehension of the review process and of the service offered to the profession by those who are willing to act as reviewers.

REVIEWS: FUNCTION AND IMPORT

Book reviews, simply defined as "an evaluation of a literary work published in a periodical or newspaper," provide information to their readers that meets a variety of needs and interests.[1] Perhaps the most prominent use of reviews is in collection development, where they are a prime source of information for book selection, but they also perform a variety of other functions. A book review -- or by extension, a review of other sources of information such as CD-ROM databases or software -- also serves as a link between the author and the reader. The reader is made aware of the author's work and gains an understanding of its content and quality. In turn, the review may affect the longevity of the book. Every word of praise or criticism can have an effect on sales, and reflects on the hours of work by the author and on the commitment of the publisher. A review can also bring to the reader a sense of new developments and research in a particular field. It can indicate areas for further study through the suggestions the author or reviewer may make, or even through omissions that are pointed out. It can provide considerations for classroom applications through the research, methodology, and materials under discussion. In essence, it serves as a medium for the exchange and dissemination of information.

Selectors know that the most desirable way to determine a book's suitability for themselves or their community is by personal examination. However, when a selector does not have access to titles, reliance upon published book reviews is a viable and essential alternative. Book reviews function both to alert readers to recently published titles and to provide them with an indication of a title's content and quality. In this way a book review serves two major functions: descriptive and evaluative. It gives a general outline of the book's contents and coverage as well as offering a critical evaluation of its worth. Besides these basic functions, the ideal book review is also able to imprint the distinctive character and essence of the book.

Quality reviewing for all types of materials has traditionally reflected the major functions of description and evaluation. Early in the twentieth century Lillian Smith, in commenting about reviewing and selecting, wrote

> a clear understanding of the fundamental principles of good writing should underlie all informed book criticism and selection whatever kind of book is being judged. There is not one set of values for one class

of book and another set for another group; there are certain basic principles which apply to all. They are best discovered by the critic or reviewer who asks such questions of a book as: What did the author intend to do? What means did he employ? Did he succeed? If his success was partial, where did he fail? That is to say, the reviewer's approach to the book . . . will be an analytical one.[2]

The terms "review" and "criticism" are sometimes used interchangeably to denote an evaluation of a work, although "criticism" is most often used in connection with longer literary reviews. However, despite the semantics, the words "review" and "criticism" both suggest an analytical response to the work in hand. Stuart Hannabuss evaluates the review process by saying

the very best reviewing, short or long, implies sound critical standards. These often impose the obligation on the reviewer of putting the work in context, indicating its significance, examining its tone and stance and the ways in which it engages the imagination of the reader.[3]

Virginia Woolf, both a critic and a reviewer, differentiated between reviewing and criticism. "The critic is separate from the reviewer; the function of the reviewer is partly to sort current literature; partly to advertise the author; partly to inform the public."[4]

Although "criticism," to many, is equated with negative evaluation, it is important that readers of reviews have as complete a picture of the work as the reviewers can provide, whether negative or positive. Reviewers feel very strongly that they have the right to submit a negative evaluation if the material warrants one. In one survey of reviewers, ninety-nine percent of those who responded felt that a negative evaluation had a proper place in the review process and that they had both a right and obligation to state this opinion.[5] In reality, though, most reviews are found to be positive, a fact that is somewhat mitigated by the policy of some journals to publish only positive reviews. The decision of some reviewing journals not to include negative reviews is no doubt influenced by space considerations and cost, but it does leave questions in the minds of selectors. No review could mean a title was overlooked, it was totally unsatisfactory or just marginal. The selector has no information with which to consider how or whether the reviewer came to a non-inclusion decision, or upon which to make informed decisions for his or her own community.

Although reviews appear in newspapers, general magazines, and the many journals dedicated to book reviewing alone, it is estimated that fewer than ten percent of the books published in the U. S. each year are actually reviewed.[6] Of those that are reviewed, a book that has received a number of reviews is more likely to be found in a library collection. Even a negative review is considered better by the book's publishers than no review at all, since it brings title recognition to the public. The importance of the collection development role of book reviews is underscored when one considers the publisher-reviews-library triangle. Many publishers make the majority of their sales to libraries; librarians in turn use reviews as their most important selection tool. The role of the review in this process is pivotal.

Beyond providing initial selection guides for all types of libraries, book reviews are often also used to support earlier decisions in those cases when a title's inclusion in a collection is questioned for any reason, but especially in areas of controversy. Published reviews can be used to help document how the title under discussion meets the goals of the collection development policy.

Since a review reflects one person's opinion or a consensus of a reviewing board, reviews should be evaluated and utilized with an understanding of the policies of the reviewing journals and the caliber of the reviewers. The optimal approach is to read a number of reviews of the same title to gain a variety of opinions about a book. This is especially critical for those titles that cannot seem to muster agreement among reviewers, but it is not always possible, as some books will not receive enough reviews to do a comparison.

THE SERVICE ROLE OF REVIEWERS: REWARDS AND RESTRAINTS

For a faculty member, the writing of reviews would seem to fall under the service category of professional responsibilities. The three roles of teaching, research and service are traditionally considered to be factors in faculty tenure and promotion decisions. In actuality, these decisions are based more often on teaching and research, while the service aspect is neglected. In a survey initiated in 1978, Kingsbury investigated faculty evaluations. Her study

> suggests that practices used to evaluate faculty members for promotion, salary increases, and tenure in accredited library

> school programs take into account only two
> of the traditional goals of most universities
> . . . current practice emphasizes teaching
> and research but not public service. [7]

In associating this service aspect with reviewing, one critic remarks, "Ignoring the high value of tough-minded reviewing, as well as the special talents and time-consuming work it requires, faculty members and administrators award little credit for the writing of reviews."[8] This attitude is reported to be naive as "one can often tell more about a candidate's scholarly standards by reading his reviews than by reading his articles."[9]

The teaching role aside, the evaluation of faculty members concentrates on publication and research because those activities increase faculty members' reputations and the prestige of their institutions. This, in turn, can lead to increased funding and support for the institution. "A preeminent reputation is the goal of university trustees, presidents, and other administrators in order to attract students, faculty and funding. This prestige is generated primarily by writers and researchers."[10]

Historically, the value of teaching, research and service as part of faculty evaluation has exhibited a change in emphasis. From teaching and service being predominant, evaluations now stress research and scholarly publishing. A closer study of this transition has reported that

> teaching remains an important variable, but
> it is difficult to assess and measure objec-
> tively. After the assumption was presented
> that research activity could be equated with
> teaching effectiveness, publishing produc-
> tivity became the overriding measure of

faculty effectiveness. Service, the third element, has virtually disappeared as a matter to consider.[11]

For those who are regularly involved in service activities, this is an unsettling reflection.

Also disconcerting for reviewers who feel they are providing service in the dissemination of information is the inequity in the indexing of book reviews. One study reports that of reviews actually published, varying numbers of them were not indexed, at least in the magazines included in the survey.[12] While some of that may be because of the inclusion criteria among indexing publications, it is important to those seeking the information to be able to locate it and for those writing the reviews to feel that their efforts will be available to the widest possible audience.

Many studies of book reviewing have recommended better review coverage of the books that are produced each year. While some titles receive a disproportionately large number of reviews, many get no notice in the reviewing media at all. In a look at the reviewing of professional library literature for 1983, Webreck and Weedman reported that

> the findings indicate that the number of reviews which appeared in the selected journals has increased over the past twelve years, but that this increase is not proportionate to the increase in the number of titles published. This suggests that the reviewing media have not been able to keep pace with the growth of the professional materials.[13]

An earlier study by Chen and Galvin reported that although seventy-five percent of the monographs were identified through familiar sources for selectors needing library and information science materials, twenty-five percent of those titles never appeared in the announcement media. Therefore, awareness of their existence came only through the reviews which appeared in the reviewing publications.[14] Understandably, one of the recommendations of their study was that the review coverage of new titles in library and information science be extended. Likewise, academic books, in particular scholarly editions, reference tools and bibliographies are less likely to be reviewed than lighter-weight critical studies.[15] Library professionals could make a difference in narrowing these gaps.

REVIEWING AND THE PRACTITIONER-VOLUNTEER

Although reviews may be undervalued for faculty evaluation purposes, not all reviewers are faculty members; many are professionals who represent all types of libraries. It is important to keep in mind not only the valuable service to the library community these reviews provide but also that there are benefits to be gathered by their writers. Reviewing can provide review authors with some intrinsic and extrinsic advantages. The in-depth examinations of the materials that precede the writing of reviews offer an opportunity to sustain and exercise critical analysis skills as well as gain an awareness of current thought and research in a particular field. Reviewing also provides an opportunity to utilize expertise and research experience gained over time and offers those new to the field an opportunity to contribute. In fact, writing reviews can be mutually beneficial. Those newly established in the profession have much to offer and much to gain. Their potential role has been recognized in the literature.

> Young and hungry beginners or near-beginners are not infrequently as much on top of their fields as are august eminences, and an editor should feel no hesitation in seeking contributions from strong 'lesser-knowns.'[16]

> Reviews offer a number of advantages for those who are beginning to develop their writing habits, want to expand their range of publications, or seek to build a scholarly reputation. . .feedback from the reviews editor offers invaluable help in improving writing style and insights into the publishing process.[17]

Although reviews are written primarily from a sense of contribution to the profession, reviewers traditionally receive tangible compensation by being able to keep the review copies which they are sent. Additionally, as typified by *RQ*'s reference book reviewers, they "receive the professional satisfaction of knowing that the time they invested in evaluating the reference book will pay off in the enhancement of reference collections or the protection of precious reference book budget dollars in numerous libraries."[18]

In most cases, reviews in major reviewing journals are written either by staff writers and their professional consultants or by volunteers coordinated by an editor. The staff reviewers bring years of experience, knowledge, insight, and commitment to their profession as well as providing continuity and consistency through their work. It becomes possible through familiarization with a reviewer's work over time to develop a trust in his or her evaluations. The use of many volunteers, on the other hand, provides a broad range of expertise to draw on as well as the opportunity to garner reaction to the materials on location from potential readers and/or users of the work.

There is the possibility that the use of volunteers can present an unevenness -- a lack of common vision or overall point of view -- so that the reviews themselves become a collection of individual opinions of varying quality and reliability. However, in her comparison of the fiction reviews of *Library Journal*, which used volunteer reviewers, and *Booklist*, which utilized staff professional reviewers, Palmer commented that

> it is difficult to understand why *Library Journal*'s volunteers better provided the information necessary to satisfy the criteria needed for fiction reviews. It would seem that professional reviewers should provide this as well as, or better than, volunteers. Possibly these reviewers have tended to make some assumptions of their own. Some may have assumed that because the reviewed titles were recommended, their audience would assume that the flow of the narrative and any weaknesses would be within acceptable limits as well. If reviews were indeed looked at in this light, reviewers might feel little need to comment except in unusual cases. If *Booklist*'s reviewers have made these assumptions, it would be unfortunate,

since readers might not always make the same assumptions.[19]

Any potential volunteer, in light of those comments, should feel more confident when embarking on a first review. Although volunteer reviewers, as has been noted, receive little recompense for their efforts, they have reported, when surveyed, a sense of personal satisfaction and have been shown to be conscientious and unbiased in their reviewing activities.[20]

In a study to determine the reviewing coverage of monographs in library science published in 1983, Webreck and Weedman examined 512 reviews written by 376 individuals. Even with one person responsible for the majority of the reviews in *Booklist* and ninety-six percent of those in *Wilson Library Bulletin*, it is clear that reviewing is a collaborative enterprise involving many committed professionals.[21] In considering the reviewers who wrote for *Choice* and *Library Journal,* Macleod could discern little difference in the content of the reviews written by the different sexes or in their recommendations regarding purchase. Moreover, the relative backgrounds of the reviewers did not seem to affect the types of comments they would include in a review. Public, school, college or special librarians, professors and academics tended to comment on similar aspects of a work.[22]

REVIEWS: CHARACTERISTICS AND EVALUATION

Reviews appear in the publication either with the name and position of the reviewer or anonymously. Those who favor signed reviews feel the inherent responsibility for content belongs to the reviewer and the reviewer should be identified with the review. Providing a listing of the professional affiliation of the reviewer also gives the reader an opportunity to weigh the authority of the reviewer and see how a practitioner in a particular setting visualizes the potential of a work for use with patrons. Over time, the name recognition of a familiar reviewer can also develop a sense of trust in the integrity of that reviewer. It is understandable that reviewers who realize their work will be identified are more likely to give strict consideration to the quality of their output.

Conversely, others feel that the anonymity of the unsigned review offers an opportunity for candid evaluations of what could be a colleague's work. The quality of these evaluations is sustained by the authority of the journal as a whole. Advocates of this approach feel that only through this anonymity can a truly unbiased evaluation occur. Despite this divergence in approach, Macleod reports that "reviewer anonymity does not appear to make for more critical reviews. There was little difference in the frequency of critical comment between the signed reviews in *Library Journal* and the unsigned reviews in *Choice*."[23] It would seem, therefore, that library professionals from all areas of specialization have the expertise, experience and ability to offer critical comment of value to others in their evaluations of new materials. They are able to draw on their expert judgment, honed over years of experience and education. Sy considers expert judgment to include cumulative knowledge, an "inseparable blend of education, research, and the myriad influences that shape one's thinking."[24] As well as the cumulative knowledge, Sy also includes as part of expert judgment job responsibilities, which widen one's expertise, and the information and impressions garnered through professional contacts and networks. Although sometimes expert judgment earned through a research specialization or intense study is needed to carefully review a title, at other times having a comfortable working knowledge about the salient points of a subject and a conscientious attitude are sufficient to advise potential readers.

Most reviews in the library and information science literature assess materials for possible inclusion in some type of library collection. As such, they should be critical and evaluative and include such bibliographical information as author, title, publisher, date, cost, format and ISBN. Although there is a lack of consensus among journals about the criteria to be included in a review, some indication as to the purpose of the book, how well it has met that purpose, and comparisons to previous editions or other books of the same type or subject area are considerations. The potential audience or type of library to which it will most likely appeal is useful information for the reader. An indication of the contents, or plot summary in the case of fiction, and degree of readability, coupled with comments on the book's strengths and weaknesses, add to the comprehensiveness of the review. Details about scope, arrangement, organization, special features, illustrations, and indexes may complete the picture, but readers will be especially interested in any characteristics that make it a unique contribution to its field. The inclusion of recommendations whether to purchase or not generally depends on the policy of the reviewing journal. Macleod, in her study of two reviewing journals, *Library Journal* and *Choice*, states that the "purpose of a review, then, is less to determine whether *any* libraries should buy a given book than *which* libraries should buy it."[25]

Reviewing is not an easy process. Reviewers are expected to treat a book fairly but submit to space and time limitations. With strict space restrictions it is sometimes difficult to fully describe reasons for reservations or criticism. The need to meet a deadline can result in too little time to do background reading, check references or make comparisons to similar works. Perhaps the personal qualities a book reviewer should strive to possess might reflect those that Margaret Hutchins described as desirable attributes for a reference librarian: good memory, imagination, thoroughness, orderliness, persistency, observation and judgment.[26] In possession of these qualities, a reviewer might be better able to transcend review restrictions of time and space.

Along with providing essential information writers must make reviews appealing and interesting to read. A veteran reviewer has remarked,

> To hold the readers' attention, the reviewer must write vigorously and, if possible, entertainingly, without sacrificing fairness. If in an effort to be judicial, the reviewer sounds pontifical, pedantic, timid, or just plain dull, the reader will turn the page.[27]

To be comprehensive, fair, and dynamic, and yet adhere to the requisite number of words may present difficulty for the reviewer, but a shorter review is more likely to be read than a longer one, especially by busy professionals. When reviewers for *School Library Journal* were asked to comment on their preferred length for a review, they were divided between the 250 word format suggested for *SLJ* reviews and five hundred words.[28] Others have suggested that it should be possible to give the essential description and evaluation of a book in less than a thousand words, although policies of the journals and editorial prerogative will dictate the length to a large extent.[29] Gail Pool describes how conflicting obligations can present problems to a reviewer.

> When I first began reviewing I imagined I would be alone with a book and my own taste and judgment. But no reviewer is alone with a book. Authors, readers, and editors all have some interest in the review and their claims are often at odds with the reviewer's. The reviewer wants to be lucid, witty, and right. The author might prefer a favorable review to an honest one. Readers want something that is interesting to read and tells them if the book is worth buying. The book section's editor wants a review that is lively, indicates the book is important (which justifies the space given to it in the periodical), and meets the specified deadline and word length.[30]

No wonder the scribe reported, "Three fingers hold the pen but the whole body toils."[31]

PARTNERS IN SERVICE: EDITOR AND REVIEWER

Another critical role in the reviewing process is that of the review editor. It is up to the review editor of a reviewing journal to choose what will be evaluated and choose who will do the reviewing. The selection of a reviewer by the editor often depends on the reviewer's competence, expertise in the field, and subject matter. Following those considerations, reviewers are selected through networks or personal contacts, or through an effort to match the stature of the reviewer to that of an author. The review editor may alternatively decide to use someone for the first time or try to attain a geographical distribution of reviewers.[32] Occasionally, books are not evaluated at all by a journal because of the lack of a qualified reviewer. Even after assigning a review to a reviewer, the editor may retain the right to make modifications to a review or even withhold it. At times he or she may discuss it with the reviewer, return it to the reviewer and request "reconsideration," or even not publish it because of disagreement with the content of the review.[33] In selecting the volunteer reviewer to evaluate a reference book for *RQ*, the section editor reports looking first for subject expertise and then

> if a potential reviewer has previously contributed to the column, writing ability, performance, and reliability also play a part . . . I try to strike a balance by involving previous reviewers with excellent track records and new reviewers who are interested in contributing.[34]

In some instances, a committee will fulfill these editorial functions and make decisions about the reviews to be published.

That the review editor decides what is reviewed can often be more important than what a review says -- especially in those journals that do not print negative reviews. All editors have limitations in the number of reviews they can print and for publishers getting the book reviewed in a journal is often the major hurdle. Traditionally, most reviews have been found to be positive and the review brings title awareness to the readers. One result of this prerogative of the editor is that the "main task of negative selection -- of determining what books librarians should not buy -- is done not by the reviewers but rather by the editors in the process of choosing which books should be reviewed."[35] Some editorial policies may help guide the editors' decisions and minimize this gatekeeping. One editor of reference book reviews attempts to provide a balance in format, subject matter covered, intended audience, price and publisher among those titles selected to be reviewed, and to also give special consideration to titles from smaller publishers.[36]

BECOMING A REVIEWER

Those who wish to render service to the professional community through reviewing can volunteer to evaluate materials for a particular periodical by responding to the published invitations that occasionally appear in the journals. Usually a profile of areas of interest will be requested, as well as information about the reviewer's background and experience. Providing samples of reviews previously written may also be required. Alternatively, a reviewer may contact a journal and offer to review for it, submitting reviews of current material or past samples. An understanding of the journal's format and policies for reviews can often be obtained from the editor or found in the journal itself. Some journals, as mentioned, use staff reviewers and consultants rather than volunteers. Sometimes journal editors may prefer to seek out a reviewer whose expertise in a field is appropriate for a needed review. Since journals differ in nature and their intended audience (scholars, specialists and practitioners), reviewers may prefer to contribute in one particular area or more than one, all the while matching review to audience. While writing reviews for local or regional publications or newspapers may result in a more limited audience, it does provide a needed service to those communities and brings recognition for both the reviewer and any institution with which he or she may be affiliated.

CONCLUSION

Reviewing is a strategic service that professional librarians can offer to their community of colleagues on an individual basis. As more books are produced today and so few are reviewed, the need exists to identify and evaluate many more titles than are currently covered. Much encouragement has been given to those new to the profession to contribute and the opportunities are available. Since most review sources began only in the last twenty years, there is an indication of a growing public interest and demand for these periodicals and their contents. Although tangible recompense to authors of reviews may be negligible, there are satisfactions to be gained from being involved and skills to be honed. At one point Katz suggested that some kind of prize or recognition should be offered to the best reviewers. The purpose of this recognition, beyond the satisfaction it would give to the reviewer, would be to highlight these individuals who are providing a valued service to the profession.[37] This recognition has been realized in the Louis Shores-Oryx Press Award, established by the Reference and Adult Services Division of the American Library Association in 1990. The purpose of the award is "to recognize excellence in reviewing of books and other materials for libraries."[38]

In a time of limited budgets for purchases, librarians need to be more vigilant than ever that their choices are appropriate for their communities. To do this they depend to a large extent upon the professional evaluations of their colleagues. If each review makes a difference to even one library and its patrons, the cumulative effect could have a resounding impact. The cooperative contributions of reviewers from within the profession are striving to achieve this end.

NOTES

1. Ray Prytherch, ed., *Harrod's Librarians' Glossary*, 6th ed. (Brookfield, VT: Gower, 1987), 670.

2. Lillian H. Smith, *The Unreluctant Years: A Critical Approach to Children's Literature* (New York: Viking, 1968), 35.

3. "Reviewing Reviews," *Signal* 35 (May 1981): 104; quoted in Grace Hallworth, "Children's Books," in *Reviews and Reviewing: A Guide*, ed. A. J. Walford (London: Mansell, 1986), 5.

4. Paul Heins, "Out on a Limb with the Critics," in *Crosscurrents of Criticism: Some Random Thoughts on the Present State of Criticism of Children's Literature* (Boston: Horn Book, 1977): 76.

5. Kathleen W. Craver, "Book Reviewers: An Empirical Portrait," *School Library Media Quarterly* 12 (Fall 1984): 387.

6. Judith Serebnick, "Book Reviews and the Selection of Potentially Controversial Books in Public Libraries," *Library Quarterly* 51 (October 1981): 407.

7. Mary Kingsbury, "How Library Schools Evaluate Faculty Performance," *Journal of Education for Library and Information Science* 22 (Spring 1982): 236.

8. James O. Hoge and James L. West III, "Academic Book Reviewing: Some Problems and Suggestions," *Scholarly Publishing* 11 (October 1979): 36.

9. Ibid.

10. Virgil L. P. Blake and Renee Tjoumas, "Research as a Factor in Faculty Evaluation: The Rules Are A-Changin'," *Journal of Education for Library and Information Science* 31 (Summer 1990): 20.

11. Ibid., 8.

12. Michael D. G. Spencer, "Thoroughness of Book Review Indexing: A First Appraisal," *RQ* 26 (Winter 1986): 188.

13. Susan J. Webreck and Judith Weedman, "Professional Library Literature: An Analysis of the Review Literature," *Library Science Annual* (Littleton, CO: Libraries Unlimited, 1986), 12.

14. Ching-Chih Chen and Thomas J. Galvin, "Reviewing the Literature of Librarianship: A State of the Art Report," in *American Reference Books Annual 1975*, ed. Bohdan S. Wynar (Littleton, CO: Libraries Unlimited, 1975), xxxix.

15. Hoge and West, 35.

16. Ibid., 37

17. T. F. Riggar and R. E. Matkin, "Breaking Into Academic Print," *Scholarly Publishing* 22 (October 1990): 18.

18. Gail Schlachter, "Reference Books: Editorial," *RQ* 26 (Spring 1987): 386.

19. Judith L. Palmer, "A Comparison of Content, Promptness, and Coverage of New Fiction Titles Reviewed in *Library Journal* and *Booklist*, 1964-1984," *Advances in Library Administration and Organization* 7 (Greenwich, CT: JAI Press, 1988), 125.

20. Craver, 399.

21. Webreck and Weedman, 11.

22. Beth Macleod, "*Library Journal* and *Choice*: A Review of Reviews," *Journal of Academic Librarianship* 7 (March 1981): 28.

23. Ibid.

24. Karen J. Sy, "Getting to the Heart of Expert Advice," *Knowledge: Creation, Diffusion, Utilization* 11 (March 1990): 339.

25. Macleod, 27.

26. Margaret Hutchins, *Introduction to Reference Work* (Chicago: American Library Association, 1944), 32-3.

27. Paul Woodring, "Some Thoughts on Book Reviewing," *Phi Delta Kappan* 63 (February 1982): 422.

28. Craver, 388.

29. George Sarton, "Notes on the Reviewing of Learned Books," *Science* 131 (April 1960): 1186.

30. Gail Pool, "Inside Book Reviewing," in *Library Lit. 18-The Best of 1987*, ed. Bill Katz (Metuchen, NJ: Scarecrow Press, 1988), 129.

31. Roy S. Wolper, "On Academic Reviewing: Ten Common Errors," *Scholarly Publishing* 16 (April 1985): 269.

32. Rita James Simon and Linda Mahan, "A Note on the Role of Book Review Editor as Decision Maker," *Library Quarterly* 39 (October 1969): 354.

33. Craver, 394.

34. Schlachter, 384.

35. Macleod, 27.

36. Schlachter, 384.

37. Bill Katz, "Who is The Reviewer?" *Collection Building* 7 (Spring 1985): 35.

38. *ALA Handbook of Organization, 1991/1992* (Chicago: American Library Association, 1991), 127.

Chapter 3

KEEPERS OF THE GATES OR DEMONS IN A JAR?

John M. Budd

Disciplines are frequently judged by their literatures. The formal literature, especially the journal literature, is the primary means of communication across the entirety of a field. In most cases, disciplines have grown too large and too interdisciplinary for a reliance on informal structures of communication. There is currently a great deal of criticism of the number of journals and the growth in this number (and not without some cause), and not all of the criticism comes from librarians. Physicist David Mermin writes,

> Most importantly, however, and perhaps most painfully, we should all think twice before writing another article. For although significant economies can certainly be achieved by channeling the great flood of papers into fewer vessels, we (and the agencies that give us grants and the authorities that approve our promotions) have forgotten that the aim of publishing articles is to communicate. The current crisis of our

libraries offers us a rare opportunity to draw back from our relentless march toward that dreaded point beyond which no information is conveyed.[1]

Even with such damnation, the journal literature is important to the scholars, teachers, and practitioners of every field.

In fact, in a time of what some would call logorrhea, the journal literature assumes an even more important place. If, as Mermin says they should, authors write to communicate, they should strive to insure that the fruits of their labor are read. It is in the reading, not in the writing, that the service function of communication is realized. If the paper that appears in a journal is read and the reader learns from the paper, is able to incorporate it into a knowledge base or apply it to a problem, then the paper has served that reader. In order to achieve the service ideal the author, reader, editor, and referee must understand the purpose of communication and work with a common goal in mind. This means an awareness that a good paper has a value-added aspect; not only is it likely to be useful to a set of readers, it may well enrich the literature as a whole by its content and its example.

With most disciplines the source of the literature is based in academe. Publishing requirements signal many submissions emanating from academic departments. Beyond the requirements, though, is the fact that many individuals gravitate towards academe because of the opportunity to conduct research and to publish. The model in the library field is different. The majority of published works do not come from library education; more are likely to be written by academic librarians.[2] To some extent there are publishing requirements for the latter group, but evidence suggests that such a requirement affects a minority of academic librarians. A recent survey by Park and Riggs shows that publication is required in only 20.6 percent of 262 institutions.[3] Their findings further show that in 41.4 percent of the libraries publication is not even encouraged. Some motivation other than the organizational need to publish as a measure of performance is responsible, then, for many submissions and published articles. The literature of librarianship is diverse as a result of the variety of practice and the minority of academics (that is, library educators).

Although the literature of this field differs from others in some ways, it has adopted some of the characteristics of scholarly and research literatures. For instance, in recent years there has been a shift to the refereeing of papers published in library journals.[4] This aspect emulates the journal literatures of other academic fields. Another similarity, for good or ill, has been the growth in the number of journals published. To an extent this has been due to an increase in the number of titles produced by commercial publishers, but some divisions and other affiliates of the American Library Association have also added journals to the field. Arguments could be made in favor of or in opposition to these new titles; attention here will not focus on the number of journals, but on the means of production -- the authorial, referee, and especially editorial responsibilities.

GATEKEEPING

The above introduction sets the tone for the following comments and observations on journal editing in the field of librarianship. As was noted earlier, the literature of this discipline is, in many ways, like the literature of other disciplines. The areas of similarity necessitate an editorial process that is much like that of other fields. One of the hallmarks of this and other literatures is its selective nature; not everything written finds its way into print, and certainly not everything is accepted by what could be defined as the first echelon of journals. There is an effort at quality control exerted by virtually every journal over its contents. The common term for this function, as embodied in the journal's editor, is the gatekeeper function. By guarding the gate, using whatever means that are common or necessary to local practice, the editor serves the community of readers. There is scarcely a pretense that the process is flawless, but diligent editors do what they can to assure that the literature reflects that segment of the field that is most serious about its work and most thorough in its execution. Beyer writes that

> editors of scientific journals perform a dual 'gatekeeper' role in science, exerting considerable control over (1) the flow of scientific information, and (2) access to channels of recognition for individual scientists. Thus, how they perform that role has important consequences both for science and for individual scientists.[5]

Her words need not be applied exclusively to the sciences; editing in the social sciences, in which the field of librarianship finds itself, serves much the same purpose.

Most of the attention paid to the editorial process focuses on the outcome. This is natural because there appears to be a considerable degree of control by the editor over what is published. There is another feature of editing that may influence content at the front end. Lacy and Busch state that

> journals are of central importance to scientists engaged in research as: (1) a resource, (2) a criterion for their choice of research problem, and (3) an outlet for their findings. As a consequence, editors play a potentially important role in the research process.[6]

As a communication tool, the journal alerts its readers to topics considered "valuable" enough to have space devoted to them. At its most efficacious this means that the pages of the journal contain the most creative and best executed work in the field. At a more cynical level it means that the contents bespeak the favored subjects or methodologies of the moment. In either case, the astute reader becomes aware of what defines success by that journal's standard. In some cases the reader may be inspired by a published paper and have a research question congeal in his or her mind because of the catalysis of reading and assimilating. The literature takes on something of the form of inquiry itself; the question is never absolutely answered; each response is just another step on the road to answer.

Even with the front-end influence, the cycle of communication is only made full by the publication of authors' papers. It is toward that end that editors are able to exert the most extensive influence and have the most potential for control. As gatekeepers, editors should also be mirrors, reflecting the standards and practices of the discipline. Beyond the gatekeeping function, editors have a voice in establishing those standards. In a sense, keeping the gate depends on the control of the destination. After all, the gate only allows one access to a place; in this case

Keepers of the Gates or Demons in a Jar? 47

the place is the community (or club) of published scholars. We cannot forget that editors are, in virtually all instances, already members of that club. Will this affect the gate-keeping? To some extent it is inevitable that editors, as scholars themselves, will have an influence over the kinds of papers passing through the gateway. Editors of association-sponsored journals (and the publications of library associations are no exception) are more likely to reflect the views and standards of the community, or its senior members. Editors of independent journals are likely to be freer to break with tradition.

Since there is a mix of types of journals in every field, there will be variance in editorial practice. Beyer recognizes this and observes,

> The degree to which norms and/or counter-norms govern the behavior of journal editors and the publication practices of journals is bound to affect communication channels and reward structures within scientific fields. It is evident journal editors must make judgments, and like other scientific actors, must rely on the criteria available within their scientific field or subfield to make these judgments. In the absence of universalistic criteria, they are likely to rely on more particularistic ones. . . .[7]

She goes on to formulate several hypotheses based on the degree of paradigm development of a discipline. Here she falls prey to the fallacy propounded by social scientists in giving too much credence to Kuhn's notion of changing paradigms. First, Kuhn described work in the natural sciences, not other disciplines.[8] His book sought to identify the means by which scientists engage in normal science and the departure that defines revolutions. Second, Kuhn himself admits that he inadvertently introduced a cloud of confusion surrounding "paradigm," which he later attempted to clarify:

> [The term] entered *The Structure of Scientific Revolutions* because I, the book's historian-author, could not, when examining the membership of a scientific community, retrieve enough shared rules to account for the group's unproblematic conduct of research. Shared examples of successful practice could, I next concluded, provide what the group lacked in rules. Those examples were its paradigms, and as such essential to its continued research. Unfortunately, having gotten that far, I allowed the term's applications to expand, embracing all shared group commitments, all components of what I now wish to call the disciplinary matrix. Inevitably, the result was confusion, and it obscured the original reasons for introducing a special term.[9]

Beyer assumes that social science disciplines can be as empirically based as natural sciences and probably assumes that theory development can progress along parallel lines. Here she makes two errors that are not uncommon to the social sciences, but that have implications for the editorial process and perceptions of it that border on the teleological. The natural sciences deal with natural phenomena with relatively fixed properties (emphasize relatively). For instance, light will have the same properties whether its source is the sun or Alpha Centauri. To this extent the natural sciences are, to use Beyer's term, universalistic. The social sciences are, because of the nature of human behavior, to a greater degree particularistic. The other error is ignoring the rhetorical aspect of all disciplines.[10] While the rhetorical turn is a part of science, it is essential to the social sciences. Its particularistic inevitability means that social science is dependent on a hermeneutical (in the generic sense) foundation. The act of interpreting is, of necessity, reliant on rhetoric. The scholarship of the social sciences, then, is going to have a different rhetorical character than the natural sciences because of the variety of examples of success. Less is shared, so the constitution of the literature is going to be more particularistic. The concept of the paradigm is not necessarily representative of a desirable goal for the social sciences; it is, more likely, a false aspiration.

Editors of social science journals, including editors in our own field, do not have a firm set of procedural or intellectual standards by which work can be judged. The job of the editor is complex because of this. The task is driven less by rules than by interpretation. Since the output -- the body of published work -- is unavoidably dependent on the editor and the editor's vision of "good" work, the literature which describes a field and on which the field is judged is a product of a small core of influential individuals. That influence is dispersed, though, as will be seen. Also, a conscious hegemony should not be presumed by this apparent influence.

THE SECOND RANK OF SENTRIES

In most disciplines (and, to an increasing extent over the last several years, librarianship) the editor does not have the sole responsibility for determining journal contents. The penchant for quality control virtually insists that more individuals be involved in the manuscript review process. For this reason peer referees are recruited from the field to apply their knowledge to the question of which papers to accept and which to reject. Ziman called the referee the "lynchpin" and stated that, because of the review process, a paper becomes, upon publication, sanctioned as authoritative.[11] While the author is responsible for the paper itself, the referee shares in the responsibility for its publication; papers do not get published without some sort of active approval. The referee's primary task is to be critical, to judge, as objectively as possible, the merits of any given paper. This is more easily said than done; balance is difficult to achieve in the course of review. Smith observes this dilemma and points out the dangers of the extremes:

> If you are not critical enough you encourage poor research, recognize and honor those who don't deserve it, mislead the author as to what is publishable, encourage disrespect for the field, distort commercial development, hiring, promotion, and tenure decisions, and perhaps actually subtract from the general store of knowledge. . . . If you are too critical, you block or delay good research from publication, waste the time of authors, damage careers, and perhaps leave journals with nothing to publish and conferences with nothing to present.[12]

Although the concept of peer review is a common one, the precise definition of peer review is elusive. Miller and Serzan attempted to establish the criteria for a refereed journal. Their criteria are probably the most detailed to appear in print and would have to be viewed as more prescriptive than descriptive. These criteria are: regularly published guidelines; regularly published style requirements; author's name removed from the manuscript; preliminary screening done by two or more persons; manuscripts are reviewed by outside experts who are not board members; the outside reviewers are selected by one or more persons, in addition to the editor; each manuscript is reviewed by two or more individuals, excluding the editor; the reviewers use an evaluation criteria form; the evaluation form is published regularly; the form, with the reviewer's comments, is sent to the author; whether there is a form or not, the reviewer's comments are automatically sent to the author; and, whether there is a form or not, the reviewer's comments are signed.[13] There are likely to be few journals in any field that adhere to all of these criteria. The last item, especially, is a sticking point with many journals. Practice is most often based on blind refereeing, and frequently on double-blind refereeing, where the author does not know who reviews the paper and the reviewer does not know who wrote it. While their anonymity is not always possible, there is evidence that blind refereeing results in higher quality review. McNutt and others state that,

> Our study suggests that blinding reviewers improves the quality of review from the editor's perspective. Editors rated blind reviewers higher overall on how well they addressed the importance of the question, targeted key issues, and examined the methods of the article.[14]

So much for how it should be; what of how it is? Bailar and Patterson offer an observation on the possibilities of peer review as it might be applied:

> Four paradigms seem to capture much current opinion about peer review of scientific works submitted for journal publication: the sieve (peer review screens worthy from unworthy submissions); the switch (a persistent author can eventually get anything published, but peer review determines where); the smithy (papers are pounded between the hammer of peer review and the anvil of editorial standards); and the shot in the dark (peer review is essentially unpredictable and unreproducible and hence, in effect, random).[15]

These cannot be viewed as discrete alternatives; there will be some overlap and combination in the editorial process. For instance, in the positive vein, refereeing may work as a sieve, but may also employ the methods of the smith in order to insure that the worthy submissions are as good as they can be before they are published. To take a more negative view, the process may operate partly as a switch, but there can be some randomness in it as well. Part of the characterization depends on the degree to which referees agree on the individual manuscripts and on editorial policy in general.

This latter factor is apparently not a minor concern, nor should it be. Glogoff examined refereeing in library and information science and arrived at some important conclusions on the basis of the data from his survey:

Only half the referees responding to the survey use an evaluation criteria form or other aid. Nearly half are unaware if the editor returns their evaluative comments to the submitting author, in spite of evidence that the vast majority support doing so. This is confusing additionally when one notes that 92 of the referees ranked "manuscript secrecy of referee from author" as the lowest emphasis when evaluating a manuscript. Why then is there such ambiguity surrounding returned comments? Over half of the referees do not know if the editor has ever acted as sole referee when a manuscript should have been sent to a referee and approximately three-quarters of the referees are not notified of the final disposition of manuscripts they have reviewed.[16]

Such findings naturally lead to questions regarding the system of peer reviewing of manuscripts. First, how systematic is it? Von Bertalanffy defines a system as "a set of elements standing in interrelation among themselves and with the environment."[17] On the face of it this seems to describe peer review quite well. The difficulty arises when we attempt to examine the interrelationships and how their dynamics operate within the whole of the scholarly community. Gordon notes that editors, in most instances, choose referees on the basis of their own knowledge and connections.[18] If this is so, there are sure to be members of the community who are excluded because of the editor's limited knowledge. This is not meant as a criticism of editors; no one can know everyone who has the potential to serve as a referee. This is especially true the more interdisciplinary the field is -- and library and information science has this interdisciplinary feature. Moreover, an editor is not likely, because of human nature, to engage someone as a referee with whom he or she disagrees or with whom he or she has a negative personal relationship. The referees, then, probably subscribe to the same disciplinary tenets as the editor.

This leads to another question: what evaluative criteria are used in determining acceptance or rejection of manuscripts? Some years ago Frantz surveyed editorial board members of six journals in the personnel and counseling field. The top five criteria, as rated by these individuals, were contribution to knowledge, the design of the study, objectivity in reporting the results, selection of the topic, and writing style and readability.[19] Coe and Weinstock studied thirty-four business journals and found reasons for rejection that have some similarity with the previous list: the paper does not add significantly to the current body of knowledge, the paper is too superficial, the paper deals with inappropriate subject matter, the paper is poorly written, and inadequate research is demonstrated.[20] The similarity of the lists and the fact that referees are likely to be known to the editor suggest that there should be a substantial amount of agreement in the review process.

The next question, then, is how much agreement exists among referees when it comes to assessing the publishability of individual papers? Expectation has two sources; surveys show that papers are rejected for many of the same reasons, but there seems to be inadequate communication between editors and referees regarding the means by which decisions are made. The result of this confusion is that, according to Cichetti and to Wong, referees differ in the issues they choose to focus on and in their substantive recommendations.[21] Further, Fiske and

Fogg found in their study of reviews of 152 papers that, typically, two reviews of any one paper were likely to share few if any critical points and that recommendations about decisions displayed a considerable amount of disagreement.[22]

These findings carry with them the suggestion that there are some less than savory aspects of peer review to which the entire scholarly community must admit. One conclusion that a number of writers reach is that bias is a reality in the review process. With any human behavior it has to be acknowledged that bias is at least a possibility, even when that possibility is recognized. Dickersin observes that bias is sometimes manifest in favor of positive results and against negative ones.[23] This may be one way that bias becomes evident, but it could in no way be considered the sole way. In fact, Sharp outlines a number of possible sources of bias in manuscript evaluation in-house:

> *For* or *against* certain topics or approaches
> *For* the orthodox and *against* the unconventional
> *For* originality
> *For* advisors (and other helpers) who put on an "author's hat"
> *Against* those whose recent papers on the same subject were accepted but ill-received
> *Against* authors who seem overproductive, which includes salami publication
> *For* or *against* certain institutions/individuals

>*Against* negative studies
>**Choosing an adviser** [referee]
>>Hoping for an answer "yes" or "no" pointing the adviser in one direction or the other
>>Known antagonisms, including those noted by author
>>Known competitors, including those noted by author
>>Conflict of interest (not just commercial)
>
>**Adviser's report**
>>Has adviser seen paper before (e. g. for another journal) or earlier, on a funding committee for example?
>>Does adviser's report show stigmata of bias?
>>Does author's reasoned response suggest bias rather than simply disagreement?
>>Does adviser declare a bias? That may not rule him or her out?
>
>**Final evaluation**
>>Bias of the tyranny of numbers. What, now, is in the journal's pipeline?[24]

This outline displays many potential areas of conflict or other causes of bias, sometimes conscious, sometimes not. The result may be, in many cases, positive bias -- that is, a willingness to accept or to give favored treatment to some individuals or institutions because of their reputations.

This willingness has even been expressed in print by Green:

> Individuals reporting a study from Stanford, for instance, hold their appointments at that school because in all probability they have demonstrable ability and a record of good research. A reviewer may be justified in assuming at the outset that such people know what they are doing.[25]

A perception of the potential for bias led Peters and Ceci to undertake a controversial study.[26] They took papers that had recently appeared in psychological journals and resubmitted them to the same journals after altering the names and affiliations of the authors and making some cosmetic, but not substantive, changes to the texts. The resubmissions were detected as such by only three journals; in fact, only three of thirty-nine individuals recognized the papers. In eight of the nine cases where they were not recognized, the papers were rejected, primarily on methodological grounds. In a similar study Mahoney had seventy-five referees evaluate a manuscript.[27] Some referees read a paper reporting results consistent with their own orientations and belief systems; other read the paper with the same data, but the labels were changed so that the results challenged the referees' orientations. The paper reporting the positive results was much more likely to be accepted. Further the referees predicted that they agree with their colleagues about 70 percent of the time regarding assessments of the papers' methodology, relevance, and presentation, while the actual agreement was more like 15 percent.

More serious than bias (as serious as it is) is the presence of fraud and misconduct in research. It is decried in the literature and various possible causes for fraud are discussed. Some claim that one reason for the instance of fraud is "big science."[28] Since World War II the federal government has pumped enormous amounts of money into the research endeavor. The availability of funding spawned large research operations at many universities, along with numbers of faculty whose jobs depend on research and, so, support for the research. The amount of money and the consequences of not receiving funding may push some individuals to less than honest reporting of research and, sometimes, the fabrication of studies so that rates of publication can remain high. Other writers recognize that any fraudulent act is serious but caution against extrapolating the acts of few individuals to all of science. Abelson states that,

> The current discussion of fraud and of deviations from ideal behavior can leave the impression of a decaying scientific enterprise. Such an impression would be incorrect. The overwhelming majority of scientists are honest and idealistically seeking to serve humankind. However, placing a white lab coat on a person does not create a saint. If the rules of the game are such that honesty is the best policy, most people will be honest. An improvement in the rules of the game with respect to authorship would create a better moral tone in laboratories and substantially improve communication of science.[29]

The above paints a rather grim picture for the journal literature. These problems, while real, should not be overstated, but they do indicate an area of concern for the entirety of the communication process. If we assume that fraud is not a prevalent condition in the body politic, we can continue with the assumption that any paper is an accurate representation of an author's work. More serious is the dilemma of bias, which is frequently less than conscious and is an ingrained part of human nature. What we see from research that has been done on the issue is that it leads to behavior patterns that are difficult to predict and that result in little agreement among individuals. What does this imply for editors?

EDITORS AS MAXWELL'S DEMONS

The editor's quandary is that the process is less ordered than might be desired. The lack of agreement among referees signifies that papers are being evaluated by a number of means, not all of which may be stated. It is expected that the process is not absolutely objective; such objectivity is simply not possible. Science relies, in part, on a two-stage evaluation mechanism. Funded research is reviewed at the proposal stage; that which is acceptable is that which will receive funding. The work that is carried out has already been assessed, at least at a conceptual level. The papers emanating from the funded research are then reviewed by journals' referees. Those ideas that were not deemed, for whatever reason, to be fundable may not progress beyond that conceptual stage. If the ideas do progress, the researchers have the benefit of the proposal reviewers' comments on which to build. In other fields, where funding is less readily available and less ingrained into the operational mentality of the discipline, there is frequently only one stage of review -- the journal and its editor and referees.

This latter circumstance, which describes the field of library and information science, is one in which there is likely to be greater disorder than in the sciences. There is no large-scale sorting mechanism at work before the preparation and submission of a manuscript, so there is greater variance to be expected at the input stage of the process. There is some resemblance between this situation and the concept of entropy in thermodynamics. The Second Law of Thermodynamics asserts that any isolated system moves in the direction of greater disorder and that whenever any two isolated systems merge the level of disorder is greater than the sum of the two. If this is any indication of the actual state of affairs of journal publishing, the service aspect of the literature is endangered. This is not an unrealistic concern; much of information theory is based on the recognition of such statistical disorder affecting communication. James Clerk Maxwell imagined a creature, though, that could defy the Law:

> Now let us suppose that such a vessel is divided into two portions, A and B, by a division in which there is a small hole, so as to allow only the swifter molecules to pass from A to B, and only the slower ones to pass from B to A. We will thus, without expenditure of work, raise the temperature of B and lower that of A, in contradiction to the second law of thermodynamics.[30]

While it has not become a part of the literature of publishing, there seems to be a tacit equation of the editor and Maxwell's Demon. This individual distinguishes between the fast-moving particles (good papers) and slow-moving particles (not-so-good papers) and sorts them somehow so that the one group appears in the journal's pages and the other does not. At times, also, it seems as though the editor attempts to accomplish this without the expenditure of work.

If the papers are the particles in motion it is reasonable to extend this metaphor and say that the authors of the papers are not cognizant of the velocity of their own papers. Moreover, it may be said that the authors perceive their own papers to be "fast-moving." In fact the authors may attempt to maximize the velocity by employing methods they see as emulating the characteristics of fast-moving particles. Armstrong writes,

> In my study of journal papers, academics rated the competency of the author higher when the writing was *less* intelligible. A possible explanation would be:
> (1) Profound thought is difficult to understand.
> (2) My thought is difficult to understand.
> (3) Therefore, my thought is profound.[31]

In any event, the paper, once written, has its velocity established and material change in its velocity is difficult to achieve -- impossible to achieve without work.

What we are stuck with is that editors cannot function as Maxwell's Demons any more than such creatures can exist in the natural universe. If there is to be change in the system, such change cannot come about without work; without work and left to its own devices, the entropy of the system increases. If there is to be change in the journal literature of any discipline, there must be effort expended to alter the various components. The literature of our own field is certainly not likely to be less entropic than that of others, so at least as much work is needed to bring about order in librarianship as in any discipline.

SUMMARY

The foregoing discussion contains some rather scathing indictments of the peer review process as it operates, on the whole, today. There is evidently some degree of bias in the process that affects what makes its way into print and what does not. On a larger scale, it must be remembered that journal publication, as a communication mechanism, is highly organized; the behavior patterns exhibited by any one journal are likely to be representative of the whole. The members of the cadre of editors and of referees are almost certain to be part of the mainstream of their discipline. This introduces another problem common to all organized structures -- the necessity of the survival of the organization. Sperber writes,

> But how do status judges [referees] evaluate the scientific ideas of those participants who provide arguments or evidence calling into question the legitimacy of the organization or the competence of the judges themselves? If these referees serve the "function" of ensuring the survival of the organization, then they are hardly likely to approve for publication those ideas that seriously threaten to annihilate it or to reject those ideas that legitimize it -- even when the former are empirically verified and the latter are

> not. . . . On the one hand, scientists who serve as editors or "status judges" are presumably committed to the evaluation of competing models strictly on the basis of their substantive truth-content. On the other hand, editors or status judges who approve of models that tend to undermine the prevailing worldview or the legitimacy of a given discipline are opening the door to the possible downfall not only of a particular model but also of the system in which the model is produced in the first place.[32]

There is little that can be done about this dilemma; what can be addressed is the means by which the mainstream submissions are judged. A number of alternatives have been suggested in the past, including the abolition of blind refereeing in favor of stricter accountability for the review of manuscripts. Some have gone so far as to champion the publication of referees' comments along with the paper reviewed. These suggestions have many detractors, however. Points brought out include the confidentiality that anonymity brings, the difficulty of recruiting referees whose names would be known, and possible reprisals directed against referees. What becomes clear from the literature is that the present system of peer review, while imperfect, is about as good a means of determining what is communicated as anything. Ultimately, it is up to readers to evaluate what is published. It should be remembered, though, that the various disciplinary fields are quite diverse and are likely to have their own communication needs. As Hargens observes,

> . . . to understand the structure and operation of scholarly journals, one must view them in the context of broader characteristics of the communication systems in which they play a part. This implies that there is no optimal way to organize editorial peer review for all scholarly journals. Recommendations about journal peer review that do not take the broad disciplinary communication systems into account may lead to less effective editorial practices.[33]

What of editorial practice in librarianship? The position of journal editor should be looked upon as one of service to the field. In order to provide that service the editor seeks to publish the "best" -- that is, the most methodologically sound, the most innovative, the most thorough, the best written -- manuscripts possible. Assistance is needed in many cases from others in the field committed to the same ideals; these individuals serve as referees. Completing the service triad is the author. Since many of the people in this field are not dependent on publication for job retention or advancement, the act of writing should also be seen as a service, sharing the ideals noted above.

The editor cannot accomplish his or her task by behaving like Maxwell's Demon, though. Work must be expended for the service ideals to be realized. Toward that end the editor must communicate the ideals and their functional aspects to referees as explicitly as possible. If a manuscript is to be methodologically sound, for instance, referees must know that their task involves the critical assessment of the methodology employed. If a person does not feel equipped to make that assessment, the manuscript should be passed along to someone else with alacrity. This possibility, too, must be communicated to the referee. The editor should expect diligence from the referees and accept nothing less. If a form outlining the specific points to be judged is needed, so be it. Perhaps most important of all is the recognition that the job of editor is important and worthy of the time required to perform it well. This will not eliminate all problems associated with the process, but it will insure that service to the entire community is maximized.

NOTES

1. N. David Mermin, *Boojums All the Way Through: Communicating Science in a Prosaic Age* (Cambridge: Cambridge University Press, 1990), 62.

2. Mary Sue Stephenson, "Teaching Research Methods in Library and Information Studies Programs," *Journal of Education for Library and Information Science* 31 (Summer 1990): 49-65.

3. Betsy Park and Robert Riggs, "Status of the Profession: A 1989 National Survey of Tenure and Promotion Policies for Academic Librarians," *College & Research Libraries* 52 (May 1991): 282.

4. See Daniel O'Connor and Phyllis Van Orden, "Getting into Print," *College & Research Libraries* 39 (September 1978): 389-396; and John Budd, "Publication in Library and Information Science: The State of the Literature," *Library Journal* 113, no.14 (September 1, 1988): 125-131.

5. Janice M. Beyer, "Editorial Policies and Practices among Leading Journals in Four Scientific Fields," *Sociological Quarterly* 19 (Winter 1978): 68.

6. William B. Lacy and Lawrence Busch, "Guardians of Science: Journals and Journal Editors in the Agricultural Sciences," *Rural Sociology* 47 (Fall 1982): 444.

7. Beyer, 69.

8. Thomas S. Kuhn, *The Structure of Scientific Revolutions*, 2d ed. (Chicago: University of Chicago Press, 1970).

9. Thomas S. Kuhn, *The Essential Tension: Selected Studies in Scientific Tradition and Change* (Chicago: University of Chicago, 1977), 318-319.

10. Michael Mulkay, *Sociology of Science: A Sociological Pilgrimage* (Buckingham: Open University Press, 1990).

11. John M. Ziman, *Public Knowledge: An Essay Concerning the Social Dimension of Science* (Cambridge: Cambridge University Press, 1968), 148.

12. Alan Jay Smith, "The Task of the Referee," *Computer* 23 (April 1990): 66.

13. A. Carolyn Miller and Sharon L. Serzan, "Criteria for Identifying a Refereed Journal," *Journal of Higher Education* 55 (November/December 1984): 677-82.

14. Robert A. McNutt et al., "The Effects of Blinding on the Quality of the Peer Review," *Journal of the American Medical Association* 263 (March 9, 1990): 1375.

15. John C. Bailar III and Kay Patterson, "Journal Peer Review: The Need for a Research Agenda," *New England Journal of Medicine* 312 (March 7, 1985): 654.

16. Stuart Glogoff, "Reviewing the Gatekeepers: A Survey of Referees of Library Journals," *Journal of the American Society for Information Science* 39 (November 1988): 405.

17. Ludwig von Bertalanffy, *Perspectives on General System Theory: Scientific-Philosophical Studies* (New York: George Braziller, 1975), 159.

18. Michael D. Gordon, "The Role of Referees in Scientific Communication," in *The Psychology of Written Communication*, ed. James Hartley (London: Kogen Page, 1980), 266.

19. Thomas T. Frantz, "Criteria for Publishable Manuscripts," *Personnel and Guidance Journal* 47 (December 1968): 385.

20. Robert K. Coe and Irwin Weinstock, "Publication Policies of Major Business Journals," *Southern Journal of Business* 3 (January 1968): 7.

21. D. V. Cichetti, "Reliability of Reviews for the *American Psychologist*: A Biostatistical Assessment of the Data," *American Psychologist* 35 (March

1980): 300-303; Paul T. P. Wong, "Implicit Editorial Policies and the Integrity of Psychology as an Empirical Science," *American Psychologist* 36 (June 1981): 690-691.

22. Donald W. Fiske and Louis Fogg, "But the Reviewers are Making Different Criticisms of My Paper! Diversity and Uniqueness in Reviewer Comments," *American Psychologist* 45 (May 1990): 591-598.

23. Kay Dickersin, "The Existence of Publication Bias and Risk Factors for Its Occurrence," *Journal of the American Medical Association* 263 (March 9, 1990): 1386.

24. David W. Sharp, "What Can and Should Be Done to Reduce Publication Bias? The Perspective of an Editor," *Journal of the American Medical Association* 263 (March 9, 1990): 1391.

25. Russell G. Green, "Review Bias: Positive or Negative, Good or Bad?" *Behavioral and Brain Sciences* 5 (June 1982): 211.

26. Douglas P. Peters and Stephen J. Ceci, "Peer Review Practices of Psychological Journals: The Fate of Published Articles, Submitted Again," *Behavioral and Brain Sciences* 5 (June 1982): 187-195.

27. Michael J. Mahoney, "Publication Prejudices: An Experimental Study of Confirmatory Bias in the Peer Review System," *Cognitive Therapy and Research* 1 (June 1977): 161-175.

28. Susan Crawford and Loretta Stucki, "Peer Review and the Changing Research Record," *Journal of the American Society for Information Science* 41 (April 1990): 223-228.

29. Philip Abelson, "Mechanisms for Evaluating Scientific Information and the Role of Peer Review," *Journal of the American Society for Information Science* 41 (April 1990): 222.

30. W. Ehrenberg, "Maxwell's Demon," *Scientific American* 217, no.5 (November 1967): 103.

31. J. Scott Armstrong, "Research on Scientific Journals: Implications for Editors and Authors," *Journal of Forecasting* 1 (January-March 1982): 94.

32. Irwin Sperber, *Fashions in Science: Opinion Leaders and Collective Behavior in the Social Sciences* (Minneapolis: University of Minnesota Press, 1990), 157.

33. Lowell L. Hargens, "Variation in Journal Peer Review Systems," *Journal of the American Medical Association* 263 (March 9, 1990): 1352.

Part II:
Opportunities for Professional Action Through Organizations

Since the exploratory efforts of the mid-nineteenth century that eventually led to the founding of the American Library Association, the need for library and information science professionals to meet together and work together beyond the bounds of their own institutions has been a central characteristic of professional commitment. Dr. Patterson's charge to his students to become involved in professional associations has been underscored by his own association activities, particularly in service to Beta Phi Mu and the Association for Library and Information Science Education (ALISE). He has also strongly encouraged students who enter academic librarianship to behave as responsible and enthusiastic members of the academic community.

In Chapter 4, Danny P. Wallace explores the problems and prospects of ALISE in the context of the association's leadership. Chapter 5, by Joseph Mika, provides a comprehensive overview of the history and programs of Beta Phi Mu. Bert R. Boyce explores the institutional commitments of academic librarians and library and information science educators in Chapter 6.

Chapter 4

ALISE AND THE QUEST FOR LEADERSHIP

Danny P. Wallace

*T*he Association of American Library Schools (since 1983 the Association for Library and Information Science Education) was founded in 1915 with ten charter members. Although meetings of library educators had taken place in conjunction with American Library Association conferences at least as early as 1903, the founding of the Association helped give definition and purpose to the growing body of professional educators.

The body of literature dealing with ALISE is remarkably small. Many authors have apparently found it both possible and appropriate to discuss education for library and information science without reference to ALISE. Proceedings of the annual conference and accounts of meetings of the executive board were published independently from 1915 to 1959 and thereafter have been published in the *Journal of Education for Librarianship* and its successor, the *Journal of Education for Library and Information Science*.[1] It appears to be the case that ALISE itself, however, has rarely been a topic of discussion at any of the reported meetings, which have focused on concerns of educators and the process of keeping the Association solvent and operational. Presumably the status of the association was discussed in meetings of committees and of the association's board, and only indirectly reported in official publications. In Davis's words, "one looks in vain for even the mention of the Association of American Library Schools."[2]

Those authors who have addressed ALISE have almost universally taken a negative view of the Association's value and impact. "In places where it is mentioned, if it is not merely referred to in polite language and briefly described, it is often the target of disparaging remarks."[3] In the words of Jesse Shera,

> For more than a generation the Association of American Library Schools has annually convened to address itself to common problems of library education, but its deliberations have been uniformly sterile, repetitious, and demonstrative of the *malaise* by which the Association has long been beset."[4]

Shera extended his criticism beyond ALISE, contending that

> One has but to attend a typical meeting of the Association of American Library Schools or the Library Education Division of the ALA to become aware of how little substance lies behind the rhetoric spoken, and how casually librarians take their responsibilities for professional education."[5]

Houser and Schrader, in their discourse on the link between library science education and the desire of librarians to place their activities into a scientific context, commented that "It [AALS] failed to perform even the minimal functions traditionally charged to such an association,"[6] and included the founding of AALS in a list of "factors [that] played negative roles of varying import and impact in the effort to establish a climate amenable to scientific research in library science."[7]

Schrader, in his bibliometric analysis of the *Journal of Education for Librarianship*, commented on the failure of the Association to adopt a leadership role, and credited it in part to the role of noneducators in determining the content of the journal. He found that "seven out of ten first authors were educators," and suggested that "the presence of such a considerable proportion of practitioners raises the interesting question of whether or not the educators are intellectual masters in their own domain."[8]

Schrader further commented on the failure of the Association to present a unified approach to developing a body of literature dealing with library and information science education:

> . . . the goal of any field is intellectual consensus, and none of the indices developed in this study point to the existence of such a consensus. There is, on the conceptual level, little interest in the philosophical foundations of library science education. There is no well-defined core of domain problems. Concomitantly, there is no well-developed core of either contributing authors, cited authors, or cited works over the 24-year period examined in this study.[9]

The tendency of ALISE to concentrate on the functions of the schools rather than on the nature and purpose of the library and information professions was addressed by Edward A. Wight:

> Since its founding in 1915 the AALS has been concerned primarily with matters internal to our schools -- standards for admission of students, organization and content of courses, teaching materials, requirements for graduation, student and faculty research, and other internal problems. Placement of graduates has been our primary external business. Our efforts to influence the practice of the profession seem to me to have been minor and relatively ineffective, and to have been exerted primarily as individual librarians rather than as an organization.
>
> Is it not time that our Association interested itself more directly in the practice of the profession? Does not the training group have not only an interest but also a professional responsibility for the progress of librarianship itself, and for the development of the stature and status of librarians? To both of these questions I suggest the answers should be "Yes".[10]

This concern with the excessive focus on what happens within the schools rather than what happens in the professional arena was echoed by Summers:

ALISE and the Quest for Leadership

From its beginnings ALISE has sought to provide a place where persons engaged in library and information science education could come together to share ideas and viewpoints, and it largely has addressed itself to the everyday concerns of the classroom teacher. Many of the articles in the ALISE journal concern methods and procedures for teaching various classes in library schools. Much of its conference program has been devoted to providing opportunities for teachers to share experiences and ideas about content and methods for teaching. This classroom focus has caused many to see ALISE as somewhat of a 'marching and chowder society' that devoted greater attention to social and self-congratulatory kinds of concerns than to matters of national policy or substance.[11]

Throughout its history, questions have been raised regarding the need for and value of ALISE. On several occasions, it has been suggested that the Association be folded into the American Library Association. An example of the motives for such suggestions is provided by Thomas Galvin:

> Reorganizing and strengthening AALS, while clearly both desirable and necessary if the Association is to continue to exist as an independent group, will accomplish little or nothing, it seems to me, to correct what Davis and others before him have rightly identified as its fundamental and chronic

> weakness -- the organizational isolation of AALS from the larger community of library educators and from the still larger community of practicing librarians.[12]

Each set of suggestions for merger, however, has been countered by arguments in favor of the autonomy of the Association, as demonstrated by Elizabeth Stone's counter to Galvin's proposal:

> I deem it [merger of AALS and the Library Education Division of the American Library Association] unwise because the personal membership of the Association of American Library Schools is composed strictly of library educators. Their vocation is education; their subject is librarianship. It is essential that library educators have an opportunity to meet together, to exchange views, to continue their own education. The annual AALS conference provides a forum to provide continuing education to library educators in relation to issues such as evaluation, subject content, teaching methods, current trends, and future prospects.[13]

Even those authors who have been clearly supportive of the Association have frequently resorted to faint praise and discussion of what could be accomplished rather than what had in fact been accomplished:

> The importance of the organization derives from its potentialities rather than from its past accomplishments. What it may ac-

complish in the future will depend upon whether it will bring its collective thinking to bear seriously upon its problems, work out appropriate solutions, and adopt new procedures which will insure a sound program of professional training. Failure to do this in the past may be largely attributed to lack of funds to insure meetings of the Association and its committees apart from the meetings of the American Library Association; absorption of the interest of the directors (who were also directors of libraries) in the programs of the American Library Association; lack of familiarity of the faculties, particularly in the early period, with the procedures of other faculties and of other professional education associations in dealing with the problems of formulating and enforcing standards; and, since 1926, the automatic admission of all schools accredited by the Board of Education for Librarianship to membership in the Association without the stimulating experience of re-examining standards and applying them in the accreditation of new schools and of assuming responsibility for constantly exploring the field. The Association has also been a closed organization and has lacked the infiltration of points of view which stem from contacts with other bodies and individuals. For these reasons, the Association has been largely unable to exercise influence in the development of the professional objectives and standards with anything like the comparable results secured by other professional associations such as those in the fields of medicine, law, engineering, commerce, and social work. Perhaps the future will witness a strengthening of its role in library education.[14]

Summers continued Wilson's theme in his statement that

The major contribution for much of ALISE's history has been providing a forum for dialogue about education among leaders and instructors in accredited programs and in associated programs. ALISE has contributed to improvements in teaching by maintaining its interest groups and publications which have allowed teachers to share ideas on an ongoing basis.[15]

Esther Stallmann, writing in the inaugural issue of *Journal of Education for Librarianship*, compared AALS to several other associations of professional educators. Stallmann concluded that

In comparison with associations of schools of other professions, the AALS seems to need strengthening for both its roles -- that of leadership in the profession at large in matters pertaining to education for librarianship, and that of the one agent in a position to bolster and assist its own members.[16]

Stallmann's comparison of AALS to other associations with similar purposes set the stage for Donald

ALISE and the Quest for Leadership

Davis's University of Illinois doctoral dissertation[17] and subsequent occasional paper[18] and book.[19] Davis provided a comprehensive history of the Association of American Library Schools from its inception in 1915 to 1968. In addition to providing a detailed historical analysis of the Association, Davis compared AALS to similar associations of educators in the fields of social work and law, with results that were largely unfavorable to AALS.

The major hypothesis of Davis's work was

> The influence of an association of professional schools on professional education is related to the level of involvement of the association with the national professional association and the professional schools.[20]

Davis rephrased this hypothesis in terms of four primary questions about the role of the AALS:

> (1) What has been the actual role of the AALS in education for librarianship? (2) In what ways has it fulfilled, or not fulfilled, its potential? (3) What are plausible explanations for the strengths and weaknesses of the AALS as evidence by its accomplishments? (4) How can the influence of the AALS on library education be evaluated?[21]

The "bottom line" of Davis's exploration of the leadership role of the AALS is stated very succinctly:

> In spite of every attempt to discount the unfavorable portrait of the Association, drawn by its most loyal supporters as well

> as disinterested observers, the decision must be reached that the AALS has not played a very influential part in the development of library education.[22]

This failure of the Association to play a significant role in guiding library and information science education is explained in terms of two "fatal weaknesses" of the Association in terms of "its identity and its leadership,"[23] which "have been so intertwined that they can be separated only with difficulty."[24]

Davis, then, joins with several other writers, not the least of them Stallmann, in suggesting that AALS/ALISE has been fundamentally weak in large part as a result of a pronounced lack of leadership. A major recommendation in regard to leadership is

> The AALS should determine to elect leaders with a capability and a desire to lead the organization, not simply to administer it until the next annual meeting. Officers, who are relatively free from regular responsibility and possess the qualities of pragmatic creativity and charismatic personableness in dealing with people within and without library schools, could give shape to the identity of the Association and generate support to implement its goals. The perennial 'organization men' and 'women', the 'wheel horses' of library education, should not invariably be chosen to lead.[25]

This need for leadership has been expressed in a number of ways:

> The Library Education Division of the ALA and the Association of American Library Schools should exert more leadership in library education and give more support to the schools than they have exhibited in the past.[26]

> The Association has not assumed the first role -- that of leadership for the profession in thinking about education for librarianship, in understanding and supporting the schools; and it has played a minor role as leader for the schools themselves.[27]

> ... library educators have always depended upon the American Library Association to provide leadership for library education. If that situation was ever viable, it surely is not now.[28]

> ... now is the time for library educators and the Association of American Library Schools to step in and fill the vacuum by supplying the leadership needed in library education.[29]

The Association has gone through some substantial changes, including the 1983 change of its name to the Association for Library and Information Science Education, since Davis leveled his criticisms of its leadership. Not the least of these changes has been the almost complete shift from an organization of professional schools to an organization of professional educators. For much of its history, including at least the period from 1915 to 1947, AALS was an organization of schools. Personal membership was allowed after 1947, and personal members were permitted to vote on matters other than constitutional amendments. ALISE is now primarily an association of personal members, although accredited schools still hold institutional memberships.[30] This shift to a broadbased organization of personal members rather than a network of homogeneous institutional members was closely tied to the decision to change the name of the Association.

> [The] Association is predominantly made up of personal members, is international in scope, its objective includes information science, and . . . the majority of members work in schools, the names of which include "information." [31]

No comprehensive account of AALS/ALISE from 1969 forward has appeared to supplement Davis's history, though it can be argued that one is much needed. In the absence of such a history, it is difficult to assess whether the charges Davis set for the Association have been addressed, and it is concomitantly impossible to determine whether criticisms of the AALS/ALISE leadership are still warranted.

One criticism of the Association has to do with the persons involved in its activities. Jay Daily found that too much of the Association was centered in the administrators of the schools, and called for more participation from the rank and file of library and information science educators.

For one thing is clear about the meeting: except for the rebels from Pittsburgh, no one but the deans spoke, and the organization deserves, if it does not invite, the curious attitude of contempt from the owner of Academe, the professors of various disciplines, who are the first to say that the Administration serves them. In the profession of library education it is the reverse. Library schools, apparently, are run like libraries, with the dean acting as the director, acting in the role of autocrat which determines policy and performance and point of view. Teachers of library service and information science need their own organization where the deans will be the observers. Otherwise the organization faces the bleak future reserved for those societies where an elite determines salaries and exchanges warm bodies like so many trained serfs.[32]

METHODOLOGY

Questions such as those raised by Schrader and Daily regarding the roles played by various categories of individuals in the activities of the Association led to the study presented here. Although evidence of leadership or its potential are not inextricably tied to professional rank, there is surely some relationship. The major question raised is that of how the differing ranks of library and information science educators are represented in (1) the official publication of the Association for Library and Information Science Education, (2) the ranks of elected officers of the Association, (3) the memberships of ALISE committees, and (4) the conveners of ALISE Special Interest Groups.

To address the first question, representation of library and information science educators and others in the official publication of the Association, authorships in the *Journal of Education for Library and Information Science* were examined for volumes 23 (1982/83) through 32 (1991-92). Articles and columns were tabulated separately. Results are given in Tables 1 and 3. Each author was counted separately, so that an article or column authored by more than one person generated more than one item of data; totals are therefore greater than the total number of articles or columns for the study period. Faculty members from programs located outside the United States and Canada were counted among "international" contributors, and no further breakdown for international contributors was attempted.

Schrader found that 90 percent of first authors for the period 1960 through 1983 were from the United States, and that Canada and Britain accounted for an additional five percent.[33] The finding for this study that only 4.7 percent of authors were from outside the United States and Canada is not strikingly different from Schrader's finding, and suggests that the perceived international focus of the Association does not extend to its professional journal to any great degree.

Authors and Column Contributors for JELIS

Table 1 shows that the authorship of *JELIS* articles for the study period was spread across a variety of author categories. Slightly more than one-third of *JELIS* articles during the period studied were written by individuals not associated in any way with a North American school of library and information science: librarians, international contributors, and "others" comprised 36.9 percent of all author contributions.

Table 1: Authorship of *JELIS* Articles, Volumes 23 through 32

Rank	Number	Percent
Dean/Director	17	7.2
Assistant/Associate Dean/Director	6	2.5
Professor	32	13.6
Associate Professor	32	13.6
Assistant Professor	42	17.8
Instructor	2	0.8
Emeritus	3	1.2
Staff	3	1.3
Doctoral Student	8	3.4
Master's Student	4	1.7
Librarian	42	17.8
International	11	4.7
Other	34	14.4
TOTAL	236	100.0

Within the ranks of library and information science educators, assistant professors authored slightly more articles (17.8 percent) than any other faculty category, followed by professors and associate professors (13.6 percent each) and deans/directors (7.2 percent). Other faculty categories, students, and staff trailed far behind, but all were represented.

Schrader, in his bibliometric analysis of the *Journal of Education for Librarianship*, noted that 71.9 percent of all first authors during the period from 1960 through 1983 were educators, and that practitioners constituted the second most numerous class, accounting for 21.1 percent of first authors. Schrader's results are given in Table 2. Schrader's concern about the role played by noneducators in the literature of education for library and information science appears to be reflected in the articles studied here.

Table 2: Occupational Status of First Authors of *JEL* Articles, 1960 - 1983[34]

Occupational Status	Articles	
	Number	Percent
Educators	340	71.9
Practitioners	100	21.1
Students--doctoral	15	3.2
Students--master's	12	2.4
Unidentified	6	1.3
Total	473	100.0

In addition to articles, which must pass through a formal refereeing process prior to publication, *JELIS* includes a variety of columns, each of which is under the direct control of a column editor. Most of the column editors act in the clearinghouse mode, soliciting and presenting unrefereed pieces on timely topics. The status of column editors is largely irrelevant to this study, since the editors rarely write the column. The status of column contributors is tabulated in Table 3.

Again, international contributors, librarians, and "others" played a substantial role, accounting for nearly a quarter of all column contributions. Within the faculty ranks, assistant professors were again the most numerous (20 percent), followed by associate professors (16.8 percent), deans/directors (11.6 percent), and professors (9.5 percent). Interestingly, student contributions (9.5 percent) were equal to the contributions of professors.

ALISE Officers

Information regarding ALISE officers was gathered from the annual directory issue of the *Journal of Education for Library and Information Science*. These data, for the years 1983 through 1993, are tabulated in Table 4. It can be seen from the table that the role of noneducators in holding ALISE offices is negligible. More than a third of the ALISE officers during the period studied were deans or directors, while 23.8 percent were professors, 17.8 percent were associate professors, and 7.9 percent were assistant professors.

Table 3: *JELIS* Column Contributors,
Volumes 23 through 32

Rank	Number	Percent
Dean/Director	11	11.6
Assistant/Associate Dean/Director	1	1.1
Professor	9	9.5
Associate Professor	16	16.8
Assistant Professor	19	20.0
Instructor	1	1.1
Emeritus	1	1.1
Visiting Faculty	3	3.2
Adjunct Faculty	1	1.1
Postdoctoral Student	1	1.1
Doctoral Student	4	4.2
Master's Student	5	5.3
International	15	15.8
Librarian	4	4.2
Other	4	4.2
TOTAL	95	100.3

Table 4: ALISE Officers, 1983-1993

Rank	Number	Percent
Dean/Director	38	37.6
Assistant/Associate Dean/Director	7	6.9
Professor	24	23.8
Associate Professor	18	17.8
Assistant Professor	8	7.9
Other	6	5.9
TOTAL	101	99.9

It is interesting to compare the data in Table 4 to the distribution of ranks among the faculties of schools with ALA-accredited master's degree programs. Although the numbers of assistant professors, associate professors, and professors in the schools are about equal, each school has only one dean or director. Teaching faculty are therefore grossly underrepresented in the ranks of ALISE elected officers, while deans and directors are greatly over-represented. The implication is that holding an office in the Association is a reflection of prior professional accomplishment, rather than an indicator of midcareer professional growth, and that holding an administrative position in a school of library and information science plays a substantial role in the election of an ALISE officer.

ALISE Committee Chairs

The status of ALISE committee chairs was also gathered from the annual *JELIS* directory issue. Data on the status of committee chairs are reported in Table 5. deans and directors accounted for 36.7 percent of all chairs, followed by associate professors at 20.5 percent, assistant professors with 15.1 percent, and professors with 13.9 percent. Again, deans and directors are substantially overrepresented in comparison to the size of the pool from which they are drawn, and the implication seems to be that committee chairs are awarded on the basis of perceived status within the ranks of professional library and information science educators, and are conferred after such status has been conclusively demonstrated.

Table 5: ALISE Committee Chairs, 1983-1993

Rank	Number	Percent
Dean/Director	61	36.7
Assistant/Associate Dean/Director	16	9.6
Professor	23	13.9
Associate Professor	34	20.5
Assistant Professor	25	15.1
Instructor/Lecturer	2	1.2
Other	5	3.0
TOTAL	166	100.0

Membership in ALISE Committees

Full committee membership was first reported in the 1986 directory issue of the *Journal of Education for Library and Information Science*. Data for the period 1986 through 1993 are summarized in Table 6.

Table 6: Membership in ALISE Committees, 1986-1993

Rank	Number	Percent
Dean/Director	142	22.9
Assistant/Associate Dean/Director	28	4.6
Professor	92	14.9
Associate Professor	159	25.7
Assistant Professor	117	18.9
Instructor/Lecturer	8	1.3
Other	73	11.8
TOTAL	619	100.1

It can be seen that the greatest representation was from associate professors, who constituted 25.7 percent of all committee memberships, followed by deans and directors at 22.9 percent, assistant professors with 18.9 percent, and professors with 14.9 percent. Although "others" were a negligible component among ALISE officers and committee chairs, 11.8 percent of ALISE committee memberships were held by "others." Faculty members are better represented as members of committees than as officers or chairs, but are not represented in numbers proportional to the population of library and information science educators.

ALISE Special Interest Group Conveners

The last category of involvement examined was the conveners of ALISE Special Interest Groups. Data for the years 1983 through 1993 are presented in Table 7.

Table 7: ALISE Special Interest Group Conveners, 1983-1993

Rank	Number	Percent
Dean/Director	11	7.7
Assistant/Associate Dean/Director	13	9.2
Professor	8	5.6
Associate Professor	31	21.8
Assistant Professor	41	28.9
Instructor/Lecturer	3	2.1
Other	35	24.6
TOTAL	142	99.9

The ranks of conveners were dominated by the lower levels of faculty (assistant professors, 28.9 percent; associate professors, 21.8 percent) and "others" (24.6 percent). Although a detailed breakdown of the "others" category will not be provided here, a substantial number of "others" were doctoral students in library and information science. Interestingly, there were relatively few deans or directors included among the conveners, with that category accounting for only 7.7 percent; professors accounted for a minuscule 5.6 percent. It is tempting to suggest that, in comparison to holding an elected office, chairing a committee, or serving on a committee, convening an ALISE Special Interest Group appears to carry very little status or prestige and is therefore a role relegated to assistant and associate professors.

IMPLICATIONS

The results reported here must be evaluated judiciously. The decision to use entries in the Association Issue of the *Journal of Education for Library and Information Science* as data for analysis was made on the basis of simplicity and expediency. A more complete picture of participation in association activities would require examination of documents in the ALISE archives, programs from ALISE conferences, and related sources of information. The documentary history that could be drawn from such sources would form a useful adjunct to Davis's history of AALS, Schrader's bibliometric study of the *Journal of Education for Librarianship*, and this exploratory study. Despite the limitations of the data presented here, certain inferences can be supported.

Boyce has suggested that faculty members at different ranks assume different roles. Junior faculty, presumably employed as instructors or assistant professors, should concentrate on instruction and publication, the activities that generally contribute most toward tenure decisions. They can be expected to provide some level of service to the school of library and information science, but their involvement in professional associations should be limited. Associate professors should be expected to assume leadership roles in professional organizations at the state and national level. Senior faculty can be expected to play a major role in campus-level governance activities and, at least by implication, have a lessened obligation to provide leadership in professional associations.[35]

Boyce did not address the issue of the appropriate level of professional organization activity for school of library and information science administrators. It can be presumed that the major responsibilities of an administrator relate to the operation of the school, and that much of a dean's or director's time is consumed in interacting with higher-level administrators, managing the finances of the school, and generally overseeing the well-being and success of the school. Although it would be specious to suggest that a dean or director has no time to devote to professional association activities, it is clear that the immediate demands of administrative duties must make it difficult for any dean or director to provide sustained leadership for any professional association.

It is clear that, at least during the past decade, the official leadership of the Association for Library and Information Science Education has been provided by the chief administrative officers of schools of library and information science. More than a third of the officers of the Association during the period from 1983 through 1993 were deans or directors, more than a third of the committee chairs were deans or directors, and nearly a fourth of committee memberships were held by deans and directors.

Associate or assistant deans and directors assume a wide range of responsibilities and the natures of their appointments vary widely, and cannot necessarily be assumed to be similar to deans or directors. Many schools do not have officially designated assistant or associate administrators, which explains in part the limited contribution such individuals make to the association. If counts of associate or assistant deans and directors are added to those of the deans and directors, then 44.5 percent of all elected officer positions were held by administrators, 46.3 percent of all committee chairs were administrators, and 27.5 percent of all committee members were administrators from 1983 to 1993.

Interestingly, although professors were the second most numerous group among elected officers, associate professors were more frequently committee chairs or committee members than were professors. This seems to confirm a pattern of higher levels of association responsibility being tied to higher levels of faculty rank.

This pattern appears to provide for appropriate faculty contributions in a number of ways. Assistant professors are well represented as special interest group conveners, column contributors, and authors of articles in *JELIS*, although their contribution is not as great as that of non-faculty authors. Although they are in a minority position in the ranks of committee members, they are reasonably well represented in that group. They are a presence among committee chairs, although not a major one, and are numerically a very minor force among elected officials. This means that the contributions of assistant professors are tangible and easy to document, which fits well with the need to build a promotion and tenure dossier.

Associate professors exhibit a pattern of maturity within the association. They are well represented as authors and column contributors, make a showing as elected officers, are the second most numerous group among committee chairs, are the largest group among committee members, and frequently serve as special interest group conveners.

Professors are also noticeable among the ranks of article authors, although they contribute less to columns. Nearly a fourth of the elected officers during the past ten years were professors. They are less well represented as committee chairs and members of ALISE committees, and serve infrequently as special interest group conveners.

The bulk of ALISE leadership appears to be contributed by school of library and information science administrators, at least to the extent that leadership is reflected in elected officers and committee chairs. These are presumably individuals who have proven their leadership ability through their institutional administrative activities, and whose capabilities are tapped by the association to provide guidance, foresight, and strength.

There are potential problems in this pattern, however, particularly in the limited role played by professors and the extensive service of deans and directors at the higher ranks of the association.

Professors presumably attain rank through excellence in some combination of instruction and research. They are rewarded for their contribution to the mission of the university by being granted the highest professional rank normally conferred. It can be at least provisionally assumed that senior faculty are knowledgeable and wise in the ways of education. That only 5.6 percent of special interest group conveners, 14.9 percent of committee members, 13.9 percent of committee chairs, and 9.5 percent of column contributors during the study period were professors implies that the advanced expertise of this group is not being adequately exploited.

The dominance of deans and directors among elected officers and committee chairs poses an interesting and somewhat disturbing problem. Although Daily's complaint about the excessive role played by administrators at the 1969 conference is surely an overstatement, the role played by the deans and directors must be called into question.

Deans and directors frequently must concentrate their energies on the larger issues of administering a department or college of a university. They may try to remain involved in classroom instruction, research, and the other activities expected of faculty members. It is patently impossible, however, to be fully effective and responsible both as a faculty member and as an administrator. As a result, deans and directors tend to experience the educational process indirectly. It is trite but true that when one becomes an administrator, one in essence ceases to be an active member of the profession. The direct experience of the instructional environment must surely be an essential component in the decision making of an association of professional educators. Although deans and directors are accustomed to providing leadership and to making decisions, they are not necessarily attuned to the needs of students and faculty. Because they are not full-time members of the instructional cohort, they may be far removed from the forefront of pedagogical and andragogical practice and philosophy.

It seems reasonable to expect that the leadership pattern of service to a professional education association would be one of frequent service in a variety of roles, culminating in election to a responsible position at the top of the association. A potential problem with the apparent leadership of ALISE, as represented in its elected officers, is their apparent lack of involvement in other association activities. Of the twenty-seven individuals who served as officers from 1983 to 1993, ten percent provided no service on ALISE committees and did not serve as special interest group conveners during same time period. Only five among the twenty-seven were so involved in more than five of the years for which data were gathered. The mean number of years between 1983 and 1993 during which one of the twenty-seven officers served on a committee or convened a special interest group was 3.59, with a median of four and a mode of five. The basic pattern during the time period studied appears to be one in which ALISE's elected officers played only a limited role in the overall activities of the association.

The elected officers from 1983 to 1993 were, however, extensively involved in the activities of other associations. These twenty-seven people held a total of 105 memberships in various American Library Association units, ranging from round table committees to the ALA Council. During one year, the president of ALISE, who was an administrator in a school of library and information science, held positions in six ALA units, including Council, two council committees, and three division committees. Officers were also active in the American Society for Information Science and the Special Libraries Association. This devotion to the profession is admirable and appropriate, but it cannot be doubted that the loyalties of most ALISE officers are split. Whether service to ALISE or to one of the practitioner associations is more important and prestigious is an open question.

CONCLUSION

There is much still to be done in exploring the problem of leadership in the Association for Library and Information Science Education. A detailed history of the Association's development since Davis's study, which covered the period from the inception of the association through 1968, would be welcome. The data presented in the present study could be augmented by examination of ALISE documents, particularly the records of board meetings and the programs from annual meetings of the conference. It would useful to extend the present study backward in time, thereby expanding the database.

The problems of leadership first addressed by Davis certainly cannot be considered solved. The elected officers of ALISE clearly operate in an environment of divided loyalties and extended responsibilities. It is not at all clear that those who provide service at the lower levels of the association have an equitable opportunity to advance into leadership positions. Those who are elected still do not provide convincing evidence of being "leaders with a capability and a desire to lead the organization, not simply to administer it until the next annual meeting."[36] This is not to say that the elected officers, committee chairs, and other individuals active in ALISE activities are lacking in professional qualifications and commitment. They are unquestionably drawn from the ranks of the leaders of the professional community. The quest for leadership for ALISE itself, however, must continue.

NOTES

1. Howard W. Winger, "AALS Publishing in the 50s: Predecessors of *JEL*," *Journal of Education for Library and Information Science* 25 (Spring 1985): 246.

2. Donald Gordon Davis, Jr., *The Association of American Library Schools, 1915-1968: An Analyti-*

cal History (Metuchen, NJ: Scarecrow Press, Inc., 1974), 2.

3. Ibid.

4. Jesse H. Shera, *The Foundations of Education for Librarianship* (New York: John Wiley & Sons, 1972), 257.

5. Shera, 501.

6. L. Houser and Alvin M. Schrader, *The Search for a Scientific Profession: Library Science Education in the U. S. and Canada* (Metuchen, NJ: Scarecrow Press, 1978), 128.

7. Ibid., 145.

8. Alvin M. Schrader, "A Bibliometric Study of the JEL, 1960-1984," *Journal of Education for Library and Information Science* 25 (Spring 1985): 291.

9. Ibid., 297.

10. Edward A. Wight, "Standards and Stature in Librarianship," *Journal of Education for Librarianship* 2 (Fall 1961): 66.

11. F. William Summers, "Role of the Association for Library and Information Science Education in Library and Information Science Education," *Library Trends* 34 (Spring 1986): 667-668.

12. Thomas J. Galvin, "AALS and L.E.D.: A Case for Merger," *Journal of Education for Librarianship* 14 (Spring 1974): 212.

13. Elizabeth W. Stone, "A Call for the Continued Autonomy and Independence of AALS," *Journal of Education for Librarianship* 14 (Spring 1974): 215-216.

14. Louis R. Wilson, "Historical Development of Education for Librarianship in the United States," in *Education for Librarianship; Papers Presented at the Library Conference, University of Chicago, August 16-21, 1948*, ed. Bernard Berelson, (Chicago: American Library Association, 1949), 46.

15. Summers, 676.

16. Esther Stallmann, "Associations of Professional Schools: A Comparison," *Journal of Education for Librarianship* 1 (Summer 1960): 21.

17. Donald Gordon Davis, Jr., "The Association of American Library Schools: An Analytical History," (Ph.D. diss., University of Illinois at Urbana-Champaign, 1972).

18. Donald G. Davis, Jr., *Comparative Historical Analysis of Three Associations of Professional Schools* (Champaign, IL: University of Illinois Graduate School of Library Science Occasional Papers no. 115, September 1974).

19. Davis, *The Association of American Library Schools, An Analytical History.*

20. Ibid., 6.

21. Ibid., 4-5.

22. Ibid., 298.

23. Ibid., 299.

24. Ibid., 302.

25. Ibid., 314.

26. Shera, 396.

27. Stallmann, 20.

28. Wilson, 162.

29. Ibid., 163.

30. Summers, 670.

31. Association of American Library Schools, Board of Directors: Rationale for the Proposed Name change of the Association of American Library Schools to Association for Library and Information Science Education. (Memorandum to AALS Members, undated (May 1982), cited in Schrader, 281-282.

32. Jay E. Daily, "A Happening at College Park, Maryland," *Journal of Education for Librarianship* 9 (Spring 1969): 299.

33. Schrader, 292.

34. Ibid., 291.

35. Bert R. Boyce, "The Institutional Role of the Librarian and Library Educator in the Academic Setting," in *A Service Profession, a Service Commitment: A Festschrift in Honor of Charles D. Patterson,* ed. Connie Van Fleet and Danny P. Wallace (Metuchen, NJ: Scarecrow Press, 1992), 150-151.

36. Davis, *The Association of American Library Schools, 1915-1968: An Analytical History,* 314.

Chapter 5

BETA PHI MU: HISTORY AND FUTURE

Joseph Mika

*B*eta Phi Mu is the only international library and information science honor society that recognizes graduates of American Library Association-accredited library and information science schools and programs in the United States and Canada, as well as graduates of select library and information studies schools in other countries.

FOUNDING AND PURPOSE

In 1936, as a student in the School of Library Service at Columbia University, Harold Lancour felt that a national honor society for library school graduates, modeled after similar existing fraternities in other professional schools, could make meaningful contributions to the field. His early efforts to involve fellow students did not achieve success and his academic studies came to an end before a fraternity could be formed.

In 1948, as Associate Director of the library school at the University of Illinois, Lancour again resurrected his idea of a library science honor society. This time his concept of an honor society was more readily accepted by a group of twelve University of Illinois librarians, including Anne M. Boyd, George B. Brown, Robert B. Downs, Icko Iben, William Jesse, Rose B. Phelps, Richard B. Sealock, Katherine M. Stokes, Lawrence S. Thompson, Arnold H. Trotier, Wayne S. Yenawine, and Madeline Yourman. Many of these individuals would later have important roles within Beta Phi Mu, in librarianship, and in library education.

With the new-found support of the University of Illinois librarians, Lancour and the librarians approached twelve graduate students in the University of Illinois library school with the idea of founding a library science honor society. Their objective was to offer to librarianship and library education a professional fraternity that would recognize scholastic achievement and provide for continued involvement of professionals upon graduation. After discussions with the librarians and Lancour, twelve students agreed to take upon themselves the responsibility of founding the first library honor society. The twelve students were Alice Appell, Jean Atcheson, Alice Cooper, Louise Lodge, Kathryn Luther, Virginia Pumphrey, Dorothy Short, Rolland Stevens, Nancy Sutton, Robert Talmadge, Francis Taylor, and Howard Winger.[1] The first officers elected were Rolland Stevens, President; Francis Taylor, Vice-President; Kathryn Luther, Secretary; and Nancy Sutton, Treasurer. Weekly organizational meetings led to the adoption of a constitution, by-laws, and an initiation ritual.

For the name of the honor society, the students decided upon the Greek letters Beta Phi Mu, representing the initials of the Greek words, "biblioteki froneos medeontes," meaning "libraries are the guardians of knowledge." The dolphin and anchor, the printer's mark of Aldus

Manutius, an early Venetian printer recognized for his beautiful editions of Greek and Latin classics, was selected as the insignia for the society. The group saw as its mission a dedication to serving others, and chose as its motto "aliis inserviendo consumor," meaning I am "consumed in the service of others," which they adopted from Friedrich Adolph Ebert's work *Bildung des Bibliothekars*.

The purposes of Beta Phi Mu have changed little over the years, with the most notable being the addition of the discipline and words "information science" that now appear in the society's publications, initiation ritual, and purposes. As in the early days of the society the purposes still revolve around scholarship and the recognition of achievement. The current purposes of Beta Phi Mu are:

> To recognize distinguished achievement in, and scholarly contributions to, librarianship, information science or library education, and to sponsor and support appropriate professional and scholarly projects related to these fields by: (a) awarding scholarships, fellowships, and research grants to qualified students and scholars; (b) publishing newsletters and scholarly works related to librarianship, information science or library education; and (c) promoting, organizing and holding meetings, seminars, workshops, conferences, and similar activities.[2]

More than 23,000 graduates of American Library Association-accredited library and information science programs in the United States and Canada, plus international institutions, have been initiated into membership in Beta Phi Mu. Membership, by invitation, recognizes and encourages scholastic achievement among library and information science students. In order to receive an invitation to membership the graduate must have completed all requirements leading to a master's degree, or advanced study beyond the master's which requires full-time study for one or more years, with a scholastic average of no lower than 3.75 (on 4.0 scale), and have the recommendation of the faculty of the school attesting to the professional promise of the graduate. Membership is limited to no more than twenty-five percent of the graduating class of each school and the individual must accept invitation to membership within a five-year period. International membership is provided in schools or programs that have membership in Beta Phi Mu as established chapters. These select schools have been designated by the Executive Council of the society as possessing criteria, goals and objectives for graduating students within their countries that parallel those of American Library Association-accredited schools. The status of honorary membership in Beta Phi Mu is awarded by the Executive Council to honor persons who have made significant contributions to librarianship, information science, or library education, and has been extended rarely in the society's history.

In its early stages, from 1949 to 1954, Beta Phi Mu was limited to graduates of the University of Illinois library school. Graduates of other schools soon petitioned the University of Illinois for membership. The officers at the University of Illinois served as the national officers for the society. In 1954, the officers decided to extend membership to graduates of other schools, conducting initiations at American Library Association conferences. With the increase in membership, Harold Lancour assumed the position of Executive Director, becoming the society's first Executive Director, a position he would hold until 1975.

A National Membership Committee was formed to assume the responsibilities of correspondence and arranging for national initiations. The constitution was revised and the Board of Governors of the society became the Executive Council, comprised of a President, Vice-President (President-Elect), Treasurer, and six Council Members who served for three-year terms. Alice Appell, Chair of the National Membership Committee, later became the Associate Executive Secretary. The Executive Council became national in composition, reflecting the membership, and meetings of the society were held to coincide with the conferences of the American Library Association.

CHAPTERS OF BETA PHI MU

The provision for chapters within the society allowed for the formation of chapters at other library schools. The University of Illinois became Alpha Chapter. Beta Chapter at the University of Southern California was founded in 1956. In 1957, Florida State University (Gamma) and the University of North Carolina (Epsilon) received chapter charters.

Delta Chapter created an international status for the society, occurring in 1957, when Lancour initiated the directors of library schools in Great Britain as members. The initiation was held at Brown's Hotel in London, England, and J. Clement Harrison, from the Manchester School of Librarianship, served as Delta Chapter's first President. Harrison was succeeded by Roy Stokes of the Loughborough School of Librarianship, where the chapter came to reside. Other schools of library and information science have petitioned for chapter membership and a list of the schools with active and inactive chapters, with the dates of their founding, appears in Table 1.

Chapters are local extensions of Beta Phi Mu composed of members organized as constituent units of the honor society and operate for the purpose of promoting and supporting the interests of Beta Phi Mu and the schools of library and information science where the chapters are located. Three types of chapters exist: school of library and information science chapters, joint chapters, and professional chapters. A school of library and information science chapter is a chapter established at a school with a master's program accredited by the American Library Association or at a school outside the United States and Canada that offers a program deemed equivalent (by the Executive Council) to an American Library Association-accredited program. Joint chapters are those established in an area where two or more schools exist with accredited master's programs, and operate as school of library and information science chapters. Chapters at schools that lose American Library Association accreditation or which close may continue to exist with all rights except the power to initiate new members. These chapters are known as professional chapters, and provide a structure for local members who desire to retain the goals, objectives, and activities of the former chapter and Beta Phi Mu.

Each chapter is designated with Greek letters assigned by the Executive Council and included in the chapter charter. Chapters are empowered to initiate members according to national by-laws and may accept into their membership individuals initiated into Beta Phi Mu by other chapters or by the national office.

Table 1: Beta Phi Mu Chapters

Chapter	School	Year Founded	Status
Alpha	University of Illinois	1949	Active
Beta	University of Southern California	1956	Inactive
Gamma	Florida State University	1957	Active
Delta	Loughborough College of Librarianship (England)	1957	Inactive
Epsilon	University of North Carolina	1958	Active
Zeta	Clark Atlanta University (Georgia)	1960	Active
Eta	Case Western Reserve University (Ohio)	designated, but never installed	
Theta	Pratt Institute (New York)	1965	Active

Chapter	School	Year Founded	Status
Iota	Catholic University (Washington, D.C.) and University of Maryland [joint chapter]	1964	Active
Kappa	Western Michigan University	1966	Professional
Lambda	University of Oklahoma	1967	Active
Mu	University of Michigan	1967	Active
Nu	Columbia University (New York)	1967	Active
Xi	University of Hawaii	1968	Active
Omicron	Rutgers University (New Jersey)	1970	Active
Pi	University of Pittsburgh (Pennsylvania)	1964	Active
Rho	Kent State University (Ohio)	1968	Active
Sigma	Drexel University (Pennsylvania)	1969	Active

Chapter	School	Year Founded	Status
Tau	State University of New York at Geneseo	1969	Inactive
Upsilon	University of Kentucky	1970	Active
Phi	University of Denver (Colorado)	1970	Inactive
Pi Lambda Sigma[3]	Syracuse University (New York)	1959	Active
Chi	Indiana University	1971	Active
Psi	University of Missouri	1971	Active
Omega	San Jose State University (California)	1972	Inactive
Beta Alpha	Queens College (New York)	1971	Active
Beta Beta	Simmons College (Massachusetts)	1973	Active
Beta Gamma	University of Oregon	1973	Inactive
Beta Delta	State University of New York at Buffalo	1974	Active
Beta Epsilon	Emporia State University (Kansas)	1973	Active

Chapter	School	Year Founded	Status
Beta Zeta	Louisiana State University	1974	Active
Beta Eta	University of Texas	1974	Active
Beta Theta	Brigham Young University (Utah)	1975	Active
Beta Iota	University of Rhode Island	1976	Active
Beta Kappa	University of Alabama	1975	Active
Beta Lambda	Texas Woman's University and University of North Texas [Joint Chapter]	1976	Active
Beta Mu	Long Island University (New York)	1976	Active
Beta Nu	St. John's University (New York)	1977	Active
Beta Xi	North Carolina Central University	1976	Active
Beta Omicron	University of Tennessee	1977	Active
Beta Pi	University of Arizona	1977	Active

Chapter	School	Year Founded	Status
Beta Rho	University of Wisconsin-Milwaukee	1978	Active
Beta Sigma	Clarion University of Pennsylvania	1980	Active
Beta Tau	Wayne State University (Michigan)	1979	Active
Beta Upsilon	Alabama A & M University	1980	Inactive
Beta Phi	University of South Florida	1980	Active
Beta Chi	Southern Connecticut State University	designated, but never installed	
Beta Psi	University of Southern Mississippi	1981	Active
Beta Omega	University of South Carolina	1982	Active
Beta Beta Alpha	University of California Los Angeles	1985	Active
Beta Beta Gamma	Rosary College (Illinois)	1983	Active
Beta Beta Delta	University of Cologne (Germany)	1983	Active

Chapter	School	Year Founded	Status
Beta Beta Epsilon	University of Wisconsin, Madison	1984	Active
Beta Beta Zeta	University of North Carolina, Greensboro	1984	Active
Beta Beta Theta	University of Iowa	1988	Active

Chapters are given charters from the Executive Council upon receipt of a petition signed by ten regular members of Beta Phi Mu, provided that the dean or director of the school or library and information science at which the chapter is to be formed authorizes the support of the school for the chapter. Chapters have representation in the Advisory Assembly of Beta Phi Mu.

Chapters are governed by their own by-laws, elect their own officers, collect dues, elect a representative to the national Advisory Assembly, and must hold, at a minimum, an annual initiation. Each chapter is also guided by a faculty adviser who is a regular member of Beta Phi Mu and represents the chapter in academic matters before the University where the chapter is located.

In the history of the society there have been professional chapters which existed in areas where no school of library and information science chapters were active. These chapters included those founded as Utah Chapter, Salt Lake City (1965), Ithaca Chapter, New York (date unknown), and Western Washington Chapter, Seattle (1968).

GOVERNANCE

The first national headquarters office was at the library school at the University of Illinois. Harold Lancour became Beta Phi Mu's first Executive Secretary and, when he left the University of Illinois to accept the deanship at the library school at the University of Pittsburgh, he also took the Beta Phi Mu headquarters with him. The headquarters office has been located at Pittsburgh since that time. The headquarters office is located at the discretion of the Executive Council, with the provision that there must be an active chapter of Beta Phi Mu in the geographic area, and that the administration of a school of library and information science has agreed to support its location.[4]

Executive Council

The Executive Council, the governing body of Beta Phi Mu, sets policy; authorizes and dissolves chapters (upon petition); reviews the annual budget; authorizes expenditures; provides leadership for the chapters through liaison with the Advisory Assembly and through publications and correspondence; enforces the by-laws; authorizes publications, seminars and awards; reports through the Vice-President to the Advisory Assembly; and reports to the membership through the President at the national initiation and Membership Meeting. The voting members of the Executive Council are the President, Vice-President, Immediate Past President, two Directors-At-Large (elected by the membership by mail ballot), and six Directors (elected by the Advisory Assembly). The Executive Secretary and Treasurer are appointed by the Executive Council and serve three year terms on the Council, without vote.

The President and Vice-President are elected by the membership at large and serve two-year terms. The Directors-at-Large serve terms of three years, with staggered terms. The President directs the affairs of the society, presides at the Executive Council and Membership Meeting, appoints committees, presides at the national initiation, and installs new chapters. The Vice-President presides at the Advisory Assembly, serves as the liaison between the chapters and the Executive Council, and serves in the absence of the President. The Executive Secretary serves as the administrative officer of the society, carrying out the policies and directions of the Executive Council in the operation of the national headquarters. The six Directors elected by the Advisory Assembly have voting membership on the Executive Council. A chapter may have only one representative on the Executive Council. All voting members of the Executive Council must be regular members of Beta Phi Mu.

Presidents who have provided leadership and guidance for the society are listed in Table 2. The Executive Secretary of Beta Phi Mu since 1980 has been Dr. E. Blanche Woolls, Professor in the School of Library and Information Science, University of Pittsburgh. Dr. Woolls succeeded Dr. Frank Sessa (1975-1980) and Dr. Harold Lancour (1954-1975) and serves as only the third Executive Secretary in the society's forty-three years of existence. The national headquarters has been ably staffed by Mary Y. Tomaino, who has served as the Society's Administrative Secretary for twenty-six years.[5] The national headquarters is responsible for, with the Treasurer, preparing the annual budget, maintaining mailing lists, arranging for meetings, maintaining society and membership records and archives, maintaining the policy and procedures manuals, issuing newsletters, and maintaining a record of chapter officers and those eligible for election as national directors and officers.

Table 2: Beta Phi Mu Presidents

Name of President	Term of Presidency
Rolland Stevens	1948
Robert Talmadge	1949
Bill Woods	1950
Dee A. Brown	1951
Helen Welch	1952
Isabelle Grant	1953
Alice Lohrer	1954
William V. Jackson	1955
Horace A. Tollefson	1956
Raynard C. Swank	1957
Eugene H. Wilson	1958
Jack Ramsey	1959
Maurice F. Tauber	1960
Martha Boaz	1961
Frances Neel Cheney	1962

Name of President	Term of Presidency
Keith Doms	1963
Stephen Ford	1964
Cora Paul Bomar	1965
Dale M. Bentz	1966
Maurice F. Tauber	1967
Katharine M. Stokes	1968
Robert F. Delzell	1969
Jesse H. Shera	1970
Frank B. Sessa	1971
Sarah Rebecca Reed	1972
Martha Jane Zachert	1973
A. Kathryn Oller	1974
David Kaser	1975
Jessie Carney Smith	1976
Howard W. Winger	1977
Esther Blanche Woolls	1978
George M. Bailey	1979
Mary Alice Hunt	1980

Name of President	Term of Presidency
Robert D. Stueart	1981-1983 (beginning of 2-year terms)
H. Joanne Harrar	1983-1985
Edward G. Holley	1985-1987
Elaine F. Sloan	1987-1989
Joseph J. Mika	1989-1991
Norman Horrocks	1991-1993
Elfreda Chatman	1993-1995

The Executive Council meets twice yearly, coinciding with the Midwinter Meeting and the Annual Conference of the American Library Association. The annual national initiation and Membership Meeting occur during the Annual Conference of the American Library Association. The Advisory Assembly also meets during the Annual Conference of the American Library Association. Membership Meetings, the annual business meetings of the society, are the means by which the Executive Council reports to the chapters its activities, the awarding of scholarships, and the installation of new chapters. Membership Meetings serve as an opportunity for members to gather in, and renew, friendship. The Membership Meeting immediately follows the national initiation of members elected to Beta Phi Mu.

The Advisory Assembly

The Advisory Assembly, created in 1976, provides additional and frequent contact with chapters, and serves as the official voice for chapter representation in the governance of Beta Phi Mu. The first meeting of the Advisory Assembly occurred in 1978, during the Annual Conference of the American Library Association. Composed of one delegate from each chapter, the Assembly serves as an advisory body to the Executive Council, provides a forum for the exchange of ideas among chapters, and forms a communications link between the chapters, the Executive Council, and the national headquarters. The chapter delegate to the Advisory Assembly is chosen by the chapter and must be a regular member of that chapter. The Vice-President of Beta Phi Mu serves as the chair of the Advisory Assembly, and the Executive Secretary of Beta Phi Mu serves as the Advisory Assembly secretary. The Advisory Assembly elects a total of six directors, who represent the chapters on the Executive Council; each director serves for a period of three years. The Advisory Assembly annually elects two Directors to serve on the Executive Council.

Committees

Members of the Standing Committees of Beta Phi Mu are appointed by the President and generally serve terms of three years. The Documents Committee is responsible for the publication, distribution, and updating of the society's handbook, which includes current information on Beta Phi Mu policies, procedures and chapter responsibilities. This committee also drafts and recommends amendments to by-laws in response to directives of the Executive Council or suggestions from the Advisory Assembly. Its members serve three-year terms.

The five-member Monograph Series Editorial Board advises the series editor on manuscripts for publication. The editor, appointed by the President with the concurrence of the Executive Council, serves for a term of five years, and in turn recommends four members to the Board for terms of five years. Income earned from the Monograph Series supports the Distinguished Lecture Series.

The Public Affairs Committee is responsible for communication with the membership, publicizing the society and its activities, and making arrangements for the Distinguished Lecture Series. The *Beta Phi Mu Newsletter* editor serves on the committee and is responsible for the content of the *Newsletter*, with the members of the committee serving to assist in gathering and preparing articles. Committee members serve a three-year term, with the *Newsletter* editor serving a five-year term.

The Nominating Committee is chaired by the immediate Past-President and is responsible for presenting a slate of qualified nominees for elective office to the Executive Council. The three-member committee serves a one-year term of office.

The Scholarships and Grants Committee is responsible for the administration of the society's program of scholarships and grants, develops guidelines, establishes deadlines, develops forms, and provides announcements of scholarship and grant availability and awards. The five-member committee serves for a period of three years and is constituted from a membership that represents library and information science education and different types of libraries and library service.

Ad Hoc Committees are appointed at the discretion of the President and with the authorization of the Executive Council or by recommendation of the membership. These committees are tasked with specific responsibilities and charges identified as having a limited time frame. Notable committees that have been appointed include the Ad Hoc Committee on Speakers Bureau, which is identifying speakers who agree to represent Beta Phi Mu and to donate speaker honoraria in order to establish doctoral scholarships, and the Task Force on the Future of Beta Phi Mu, which addressed the broadening of the scope of Beta Phi Mu to include information science/studies, undergraduate studies, and other future roles of the society.

Association of College Honor Societies

Beta Phi Mu's status as a national honor society was recognized in 1968 when it was admitted to membership in the Association of College Honor Societies (ACHS). The objective of the ACHS is to encourage honor societies in the establishment and maintenance of desirable standards and useful functions in higher education. As a member of ACHS, Beta Phi Mu upholds the purposes of an honor society, which are to encourage and recognize superior scholarship and/or leadership achievement in its particular field or profession. Beta Phi Mu is one of only fifty-seven honor societies that have achieved membership and recognition by the Association of College Honor Societies.

Beta Phi Mu national and chapters hold tax exempt status, under section 501 (c) 3 of the Internal Revenue Code. The society does not discriminate against or in favor of any member on account of race, religion, creed, national origin, political belief, sex or sexual orientation, or age. Beta Phi Mu also subscribes to the principles of intellectual freedom for its members, and for its recipients of scholarships and grants as individuals, but does not endorse any position promulgated, any political activity engaged in, or any cause espoused by its members or recipients of scholarship and grants.

SCHOLARSHIPS AND AWARDS

Beta Phi Mu has created scholarship awards encouraging basic professional study for individuals desiring to enter library and information studies and continuing education opportunities for Beta Phi Mu members.

The Sarah Rebecca Reed Scholarship

In 1978, the Executive Council decided to name tuition scholarships for individuals beginning library training in an American Library Association-accredited library program in honor of Sarah Rebecca Reed, a former teacher, librarian, and director of the School of Library Science at Emporia State College (Kansas) who died in 1978. She was the 25th President of Beta Phi Mu. A respected scholar and educator, she was honored in 1968 by the American Library Association and by Beta Phi Mu with the Award for Distinguished Service to Education for Librarianship. This dynamic leader was characterized as one for whom "there was no such thing as impossible," and who, "through leadership of rare excellence . . . made a permanent contribution to humanity. Therein lies her immortality." Awarded annually in the spring, the Sarah Rebecca Reed Scholarship is given to a student beginning library or information science studies at an American Library Association-accredited school. Criteria considered for awarding the scholarship include undergraduate and graduate grade point average, work experience, the applicant's ability to undertake graduate study, motivation for professional study, and potential for the profession of librarianship.

Prior to 1978, the beginning scholarship award winners were A. Denise Farrugia (1976), Roberta Blitz (1976), Rebecca Gonzalez (1977), Valerie Andersen

(1977), and William Serban (1977). Since 1978 the Sarah Rebecca Reed Scholarship has been awarded to David Guillory (1978), Charles Julian (1978), Jo Ann Fisher (1979), Karen Leigh Sinkule (1979), David D. Fleckenstein (1980), Catherine Lord Cain (1981), Michael Craig Piper (1981), Carol A. Morgan (1982), Christopher W. Nolan (1982), Sara Louise McGill (1983), Jean R. Lewis (1984), Terri Lynn Holsten (1985), Cynthia Rasely (1986), Tina B. Bixler (1986), Lindsay D. Ruth (1987), Victor Liu (1988), Jennifer Crawford (1988), Sharilyn Smith (1988), Mary Colleen Deignan (1990), Ann B. Kratz (1991), Lee Anne Hagewood (1992), and Julie Ann Stoner (1992).

The Frank B. Sessa Scholarship

The Frank B. Sessa Scholarship is awarded to Beta Phi Mu members to encourage continuing education experiences. The Continuing Education Scholarship begun in 1976 was renamed in 1980 to honor Emeritus Professor Frank B. Sessa (1911-1987) of the School of Library and Information Science at the University of Pittsburgh. Sessa, who served as Director of the Miami Public Library, was the 26th President of Beta Phi Mu, and served as Beta Phi Mu Executive Secretary from 1975 to 1980. Continuing education scholarships are awarded on the basis of a plan of study, usefulness of the planned study to the applicant's present job, and/or usefulness of the planned study to the applicant's future. Winners have included Patricia Ann Hooten (1976), Margot S. Krissiep (1978), William H. Roberson (1978), Ann Carlson (1979), Ruth M. Free (1980), Sylvia C. Mitchell (1980), Francis Miksa (1983), Connie Champlin (1986), Joan Repp (1987), Marion T. Reid (1989), Sr. Lauretta McCusker (1991), and Charlotte A. Caley (1992). The award was not presented in 1977, 1981, 1982, 1984, 1985, 1988, and 1990.

The Harold Lancour Scholarship for Foreign Study

The Harold Lancour Scholarship for Foreign Study was first awarded in 1976 and is available to an information professional interested in conducting a research project. This scholarship is named in honor of Dr. Lancour (1908-1981), who was one of the founders of Beta Phi Mu, served as its Executive Secretary for twenty-five years, and was Dean Emeritus of the Graduate School of Library and Information Science at the University of Pittsburgh. Dr. Lancour encouraged an international student body and served as a consultant to institutions and organizations in England, France, Mali, Guatemala, Iran, Chile, Nigeria, and Wales. He was also one of the founders and first editor of the *Journal of Education for Librarianship* and managing editor for the first ten years of *Library Trends*. The scholarship was initiated by Beta Phi Mu to contribute to international understanding, to permit interested librarians or library and information science school students to survey foreign libraries or library programs, to attend an international library and information science program for a short period of time, and/or to conduct library and information science research in a foreign country. Scholarships are awarded on the basis of a plan of study or research, and usefulness of the study or research to the applicant and to the profession. Winners of the Lancour Scholarship have included Miles M. Jackson (1976), Katherine Cveljo (1978), Judy Komor (1979), Wayne A. Wiegand (1981), Victor F. Marx (1982), Mary Niles Maack (1983), Ann F. Donovan (1984), John V. Richardson, Jr. (1986), Pamela Spence Richards (1988), Martha L. Brogan (1989), Ron Chepesiuk (1989), Maureen White (1990), Lori D. Foulke (1991), and Eric A. Johnson (1992). The Lancour scholarship was not awarded in 1977, 1980, 1985, and 1987.

The Beta Phi Mu Award

Beta Phi Mu sponsors the Beta Phi Mu Award to further the society's goals of promoting excellence in teaching and the development of better educational programs. The award recognizes distinguished service in the field of library and information science education. The award winner was initially chosen by Beta Phi Mu, but in 1956 the Executive Council decided to have the award conferred through the American Library Association. Nominations are made to the awards committee of the American Library Association, and are not restricted to library and information science faculty or professionals, but may include anyone who has made an outstanding contribution to education for library and information science through tools, methods, or classroom techniques. The Beta Phi Mu Award consists of a cash award and citation, and is presented at the American Library Association Annual Conference. Winners of the Beta Phi Mu Award have included Rudolph H. Gjelsness (1954), Gretchen Knief Schenk (1955) Margaret I. Rufsvold (1956), Lucy M. Crissey (1957), Florence Van Hoesen (1958), Anita M. Hostetter (1959), Louis Round Wilson (1960), Robert L. Gitler (1961), Florrinell F. Morton (1962), Ernest J. Reece (1963), Charles C. Williamson (1964), Jesse H. Shera (1965), Rev. James Joseph Kortendick (1966), Louis Shores (1967), Sarah Rebecca Reed (1968), Ethel M. Fair (1969), Raynard C. Swank (1970), Leon Carnovsky (1971), Margaret E. Monroe (1972), Lester Asheim (1973), Martha T. Boaz (1974), Kenneth R. Shaffer (1975), Carolyn I. Whitenack (1976), Russell E. Bidlack (1977), Frances E. Henne (1978), Conrad Henry Rawski (1979), Virginia Lacy Jones (1980), Haynes McMullen (1981), David K. Berninghausen (1982), J. Periam Danton (1983), Jane Anne Hannigan (1984), Robert M. Hayes

(1985), Agnes Lytton Reagan (1986), Sarah Katherine Vann (1987), Samuel Rothstein (1988), Charles D. Patterson (1989), Robert D. Stueart (1990), Edward G. Holley (1991), and Guy Garrison (1992).

Special Awards

Beta Phi Mu has made special awards in the past to honor individuals who have provided service to the profession, library education and to the society. In 1973, special posthumous awards were given in memory of Patricia B. Knapp of Wayne State University and Ralph R. Shaw of Rutgers University. Elizabeth W. Stone was recognized for her work in library and information science education and continuing education with a Certificate of Distinction in 1976. A special memorial award was given in 1982 in tribute to the many contributions of Dr. Harold Lancour.

For a short time Beta Phi Mu also awarded the Beta Phi Mu Good Teaching Award, given for excellence in teaching and limited to those engaged in full-time teaching. Winners of this discontinued award included Frances Neel Cheney, Mate Graye Hunt, Ann Ethlyn Markley, Mary V. Gaver, Seymour Lubetzky, and Evalene P. Jackson. The Beta Phi Mu Award for Excellence in Professional Writing was provided by a grant from United Educators, Incorporated and was first given in 1960. The award was given to library and information science students for excellent writing and suitability for publication as judged by a committee of editors of professional journals. Recipients of this award were K. Ramakrishna Rao, Alfred H. Wuester, William R. Woods, John A. Colson, Betty Callaham, Joseph H. Derbyshire, Helen H. Shelton, Raymond Yamachika, Herbert Hoffman, and David E. Eisenman.

PUBLICATION PROGRAM

Beta Phi Mu sponsors a diverse publications series. Since its inception the society has published the *Beta Phi Mu Newsletter*, which is the principal communication vehicle for the membership, chapters, and officers.

The Chapbook Series
Between 1953 and 1983, Beta Phi Mu published a Chapbook Series consisting of limited and attractive editions intended to combine text and format in the interest of graphic arts and topics of interest to information professionals. Ralph Eckerstrom, a book designer at the University of Illinois Press, sparked the concept of the Chapbook Series while speaking at the 1950 initiation banquet. Following his presentation the Beta Phi Mu officers decided to publish a series in which designers would be free to be as creative in their publications as possible.

Ralph Eckerstrom's address became Chapbook Number One. Eight hundred copies of *Contemporary Book Design* were published in 1953. Chapbook One is a presentation of modern trends in book design by a consistent winner of graphic arts prizes. Eckerstrom retained his affiliation with Beta Phi Mu, agreeing to be the Chapbook Series designer. The first Publications Committee consisted of Dee A. Brown, Helen Welch Tuttle, Ralph McCoy, and Harold Lancour. Tuttle served as the first editor for a period of twenty-two years, during which eleven Chapbooks were published.

Chapbook Two (1956), *Fine Binding in America: The Story of the Club Bindery*, by E. A. Thompson and Lawrence A. Thompson provides a close-up view of the colorful bibliophiles who founded the Club Bindery.

Chapbook Three (1957), *Desert Daisy*, by H. G. Wells, is a facsimile of a story written in a notebook when Wells was a boy. This Chapbook was chosen as one of the Fifty Best Books of the year by the American Institute of Graphic Arts in 1957, and was a Top Honor Book in the Ninth Annual Chicago Book Clinic Show.

Chapbook Four (1960), *The Odyssey of a Film-Maker*, by Francis Hubbard Flaherty, describes the life of Robert Flaherty, creator of *Nanook*, *Moana*, *Man of Aran*, and *Louisiana Story*, as told by his wife. The work, designed by Bert Clarke, was a Top Honor Book in the Fifth Annual Midwestern Books Competition, and received a Certificate of Special Merit in the Nineteenth Exhibition of Printing of the New York Employing Printers Association.

Chapbook Five/Six (1962), *Mr. Macready Produces As You Like It: A Prompt-Book Study*, edited by Charles H. Shattuck, is a facsimile edition of a 19th century prompt-book with notes and illustrations. It won a place in the Eighth Annual Midwestern Books Competition and was included in *Saturday Review*'s "Pick of St. Nick."

Chapbook Seven (1964), *The Confederate Hundred*, written by Richard Harwell and designed by Fred Anthoensen, is a select bibliography of Confederate imprints with annotations written at the time the books were first published.

Chapbook Eight (1967), *Raking the Historic Coals: The A.L.A. Scrapbook of 1876*, by Edward G. Holley, is a history of the founding of the American Library Association, published ninety-one years after the first conference of librarians was held in Philadelphia, Pennsylvania. It was selected as a Top Honor Book in the 19th Annual Chicago Book Clinic Exhibition for 1967 publications.

Chapbook Nine (1972), *Browning's Old Schoolfellow*, by Jack Herring, is a reproduction of a series of sketches by the father of Robert Browning together with a search of the poet's work for the father's influence. It was chosen as one of Fifty Best Books of the Year.

Chapbook Ten (1974), *The Three Voyages of Captain Cook*, by Frank Paluka, is a narrative of the three Cook voyages based on a careful sifting and collation of a dozen or more first-hand accounts. The book was designed by Michael Stancik of R. R. Donnelley and was designated a Top Honor Book in the Chicago Book Clinic Design Competition for 1975.

Chapbook Eleven (1975), *Salmagundi: Byron, Allegra, and the Trollope Family*, written by N. John Hall and designed by P. J. Conkwright, is a satiric poem by Fanny Trollope and the story of how it came to be written, involving such personages as Byron, Shelley, and Anthony Trollope.

Chapbook Twelve (1977), *The Library at Mt. Vernon*, by Frances Laverne Carroll and Mary Meacham, describes George Washington's home library, what he collected, how he obtained books, and how he used them.

Chapbook Thirteen (1979), *The History of a Hoax: Edmund Lester Pearson, John Cotton Dana, and the Old Librarian's Almanack*, by Wayne A. Wiegand, is the story of an elaborate joke designed as a spoof on librarianship in 1909 by Edmund Lester Pearson, librarian-turned-writer, and John Cotton Dana.

Chapbook Fourteen (1980), *A Book for a Sixpence: The Circulating Library in America*, written by David Kaser and designed by Bruce Campbell, is a history of the circulating library in 18th and 19th century America.

Chapbook Fifteen (1981), *Books for Sammies: The American Library Association and World War I*, by Arthur

P. Young, is a definitive study of the American Library Association's activities during World War I. Two appendices of interest list the major Army and Navy camp libraries between 1917 and 1919, plus books and pamphlets banned by the War Department. Design specifications were provided by Glenn House, Director of the Gorgas Oak Press (Alabama).

Chapbook Sixteen (1983), *Leaders in American Librarianship, 1925-1975*, by Wayne A. Wiegand, is a compilation of essays on prominent academic library leaders over the past half century written by fifteen library historians. This Chapbook was the last entry in the Chapbook Series.

Chapbooks One through Fourteen are out-of-print. Chapbook Fifteen is available from the national office of Beta Phi Mu. In 1983, Beta Phi Mu ceased to act as its own publisher and contracted with other publishers to produce its publications. Chapbook Sixteen is available from the Publishing Services Division of the American Library Association.

The Monograph Series

In 1986, the Executive Council approved the inauguration of the Beta Phi Mu Monograph Series to replace the Chapbook Series. The society also has entered into an agreement with a commercial press to assume retail sales and distribution of future numbers. Since 1987, Greenwood Press has been the distributor for the series. Publications in the Monograph Series consist of book-length scholarly works based on original research in subjects of interest to library and information professionals. Wayne Wiegand served as editor for the first three Monographs. Titles published to date include:

Wayne Wiegand, *"An Active Instrument for Propaganda:" The American Public Library During World War I.* Beta Phi Mu Monograph No. 1 (New York: Greenwood, 1989).

Phyllis Dain and John Y. Cole, eds., *Libraries and Scholarly Communication in the United States: The Historical Dimension.* Beta Phi Mu Monograph No. 2 (New York: Greenwood, 1990).

Robyn Hansen, ed., *At Home With a Book: Reading in America, 1840-1940.* Beta Phi Mu Monograph No. 3 (New York: Greenwood, 1992).

Beta Phi Mu has entered into association with *Library and Information Science Research* to provide a communication vehicle for the society, as well as a membership perquisite. New initiates for many years have received a copy of one of the Chapbooks as a gift from the national headquarters. With the adoption of the Monograph Series as the publication series, Chapbooks will no longer be available. The Executive Council has negotiated with a recognized professional scholarly journal which to provide space for the society to communicate its activities or news, and to also provide scholarly and professional information to members. The first-year subscription is to be provided as a gift to initiates. With the adoption of *Library and Information Science Research* as one means for scholarly publication, Beta Phi Mu has again manifested its concern for research and scholarship.

OTHER PROGRAMS

The society has also expressed interest in library education in other forms. It has sponsored conferences, sometimes as joint ventures with other groups. In 1976, Beta Phi Mu provided a grant to the *Journal of Library History* and was assisted by the American Library History Round Table of the American Library Association in co-sponsoring Library History Seminar V, from October 3-6, 1976, at Philadelphia's Hilton Hotel. Participants heard some of the profession's most distinguished lecturers discuss various phases of American library history and toured historic libraries. Beta Phi Mu also provided travel grants for eight participants in the Seminar. The society also provided partial support for Library History Seminar VI in 1980. In 1976, Beta Phi Mu expressed its ongoing commitment to intellectual freedom through a $12,000 gift to the American Library Association Intellectual Freedom Committee as a contribution to its First Amendment film project.

A subsidy from Beta Phi Mu helped in the founding of the *Journal of Education for Librarianship*. In 1978, a special meeting for Beta Phi Mu members was held in Edmonton at the Canadian Library Association Conference.

From its beginning until 1987, Beta Phi Mu utilized an initiation ritual which was written by the founding members and revised in 1975. In 1987, to reflect the emergence and importance of information studies, a new initiation ritual was approved by the Executive Council and formally approved by the membership in 1988. The ritual was authored by Edward G. Holley, and was first used at in 1987 during the national initiation held at the Mechanics Institute Library, San Francisco.

CONCLUSION

Beta Phi Mu continues to grow through membership and is actively involved in scholarly publishing, the awarding of scholarships, and similar honor society activities. It maintains the high ideals established at its founding as is expected of an honor society.

This chapter is appropriately placed in this volume to recognize the talents, energy, devotion, and work Dr. Charles Patterson has given to Beta Phi Mu. Over the years Dr. Patterson has been a representative for the Beta Zeta Chapter of Louisiana State University to the Advisory Assembly, served as Faculty Representative for the Louisiana State University chapter, and served as a Director on the Executive Council. In 1989, he was named recipient of the Beta Phi Mu Award.

NOTES

1. The author is indebted to Alice Appell who recorded the founding of the society and whose presence at the beginning of the honor society is recorded in her article on Beta Phi Mu in the *Encyclopedia of Library and Information Science*, (New York: M. Dekker, 1969, volume 2, pages 347-350) and upon which the formative history of this chapter is based; to Mary Tomaino, Administrative Secretary of Beta Phi Mu; and to E. Blanche Woolls, Executive Director, who provided access to, and information from, the society archives.

2. *Beta Phi Mu Handbook*, edition under revision, 1991.

3. Pi Lambda Sigma, a library science honor society existing at Syracuse University, became a chapter of Beta Phi Mu in 1959, and was chartered into Beta Phi Mu under its own name.

4. The national headquarter's address is: Beta Phi Mu, School of Library and Information Science, University of Pittsburgh, LIS Building, Pittsburgh, PA 15260; (412)624-9439.

5. Mary Tomaino retired in 1992; at this writing, the society is currently conducting a search for her replacement.

Chapter 6

THE INSTITUTIONAL SERVICE ROLE OF THE LIBRARIAN AND LIBRARY AND INFORMATION SCIENCE EDUCATOR IN THE ACADEMIC SETTING

Bert R. Boyce

Service is the third leg of the triad of a typical university's mission, and normally it is the least well defined and the least likely to receive priority treatment from faculty or administration. This lack of definition can lead to real problems in discussions of the importance of institutional service in the academic setting.

Difficulties arise in studying the influence of professional service on research performance because professional service can mean so many things. Service may include local campus committee work, refereeing publications for journals, reviewing grant proposals, consulting, and holding office in a professional association. Service to local-campus committees and disciplinary associations could have opposite effects on research performance.[1]

Prior to any discussion of the priority of the service role in the academic setting, a clear categorization of the activities that make up that role seems necessary. Any such categorization seems more or less arbitrary. Broadly speaking, service can be divided into on-campus and off-campus service. Off-campus service can be either to the journals or associations of a discipline or profession, in which case the university normally supports the faculty member's time (although some expenses may be covered), or it can be a commercial activity such as consulting or editing. In the latter case the faculty member is operating a small business with university compliance and often with direct university support. The term "public service" can be used to cover both of these activities. It could also be utilized to denote community service to church groups, charities, or service clubs, but such service is not normally a direct part of an academic institution's mission, and is considered a voluntary activity.

On-campus or institutional service, which is normally some form of faculty governance activity, may also be usefully split into two segments, not on the basis of any strikingly different form of activity, but rather on the basis of the domain of that activity. Service in the academic department and service outside the academic department can constructively be viewed separately since faculty have different motivations for participating in them, and the results of this participation may have different effects on other activities and on a unit's power base.

SERVICE AND THE LIBRARY FACULTY

In the academic setting the librarian, whether in the library of an elementary school or in the director's chair in a major research university, has service responsibilities that go beyond those associated with the professional activity of providing information services to a clientele. These local responsibilities have to do with the governance of the institution, which in academic settings is, at least in part, a role played by the faculty. The library and information science educator and the librarian with faculty status will have the same service responsibilities as any other faculty member. Institutional service includes service to students, colleagues, the department, and the organization as a whole. Such responsibilities are normally fulfilled through membership in committees, senates, councils, and other campus groups. They may also involve advising student groups and consulting in specialty areas within the institution. Faculty governance implies that faculty members are active participants in the formulation of policy and the administration of the institution. These are time-consuming activities with limited rewards and recognition. Promotion, retention and tenure documents nearly always discuss service as a critical element, but only in the rare case define just what activities count and what their relative importance might be.

PUBLIC SERVICE

The library community tends to think of service in terms of public service rather than service to an academic institution, and of public service primarily as work within professional associations. There is certainly no shortage of participation in such organizations among librarians and library and information science faculty. In fact, it has been asserted that such service may be excessive.[2] Heim has suggested that public service should be tied to research activity if it is to have value in the academic environment.

> . . . if faculty do take on public service responsibilities it must be public service that is grounded in their primary assignment -- the production of new knowledge through research. Public service activities should be judged by the degree to which the expertise of the faculties in research methodologies are brought to bear on the profession's concerns.[3]

One can certainly argue that such participation is of primary benefit to the faculty member in that it provides a way of staying current with problems and practice in the field.[4]   Both these positions, however, suggest that professional service should not be valued in and of itself by an institution of learning, but rather esteemed for the added significance it can bring to the other missions, research and teaching. While all three are certainly interrelated, it nonetheless seems clear from their published statements that such institutions value public service for itself, and not exclusively for its side benefits to research and teaching.

While public service is certainly a well accepted part of a university's mission today, it was not always so. In 1975 Lewis made the case for the inappropriateness of a public role by basically ignoring service of all kinds in his discussion on merit in academia, except to state,

> In their attempt to win public -- and financial -- support, academic administrators have allowed universities to assume more and more functions not central to education. The drift has reached the point where many universities now acknowledge that they have three equally relevant functions -- teaching,

research, and *community service*. But just as the emphasis on instruction perhaps fosters the social ethic and the emphasis on research fosters individualism, the accent on service promotes bureaucracy.[5]

Devastating criticism indeed, but not, it seems, a major concern of the modern university. It thus appears that public service is an appropriate activity for librarians in the academic environment, and certainly for faculty of schools of library and information science. It seems clear that it is perceived as such by most of the field. Any controversy that exists concerns either motivation or the extent to which such service may detract from other activities.

THE RATIONALE FOR INSTITUTIONAL SERVICE

Institutional service is not subject to this sort of controversy. Its significance to the institution is obvious if some mechanism for faculty governance of the academic function of the institution is to be maintained. What is less clear is the value placed upon such participation by academic administrators, retention, tenure and promotion committees, faculty and librarians. It seems clear that all these groups would rate service, whether institutional or external, well behind teaching and research in the evaluation of their subordinates. One study that ranks the criteria for tenure for academic librarians finds service not only to be of least significance, but to be declining in importance over time.[6] In Kingsbury's look at faculty performance evaluation, institutional service receives no weight in the dean's and director's criteria, and activity in professional associations ranks fifth in the six criteria in use.[7] In his study of faculty preferences for job related activities Bess finds that off campus service activities do not rank high, and that on campus governance type services rate lowest of all.[8] On the other hand, Seldin, in his survey of more than six hundred academic deans in liberal arts colleges outside a university environment, finds campus committee work is the third most important factor in faculty evaluation, preceded only by classroom teaching and student advising.[9] There does not appear to be a clear mandate or strong incentive for participation in University governance in place.

Strikingly, however, for library and information science faculty the value of such participation should be clear indeed. In her work on closings of schools of library and information science, Paris finds that the lack of links to other units of the university is a significant constant in school's profiles prior to their demise.[10] The information available on the more recent closings strongly reinforces this finding. Regular participation in university-wide service activities establishes just those connections that may be necessary for survival. It may well be that administrators of schools of library and information science should place as much emphasis on institutional service as they do on public service and perhaps more. Gamble has argued that academic librarians should do so as well.[11] Her reasons apply to schools of library and information science as well to academic libraries.

Both academic libraries and schools of library and information science can easily become isolated from the process of academic governance, and isolation leads to a perception not only of non-involvement but of the appropriateness of such non-involvement. Such a perception is a very short step from a classification as inferior to other faculties. It is surprisingly easy for faculty and administrators to view library activities as essentially clerical, and to form no clear picture as to their role in the educational process, or of the role of the information professional in that process. It is not a difficult leap from unfamiliar to unnecessary when decisions must be made on the redistribution of resources.

Heim and Ostertag have suggested six sources of institutional power that may be utilized by academic divisions, and particularly schools of library and information science, to ensure survival and win influence and resources.[12] These are Centrality, Excellence, External Support, Field Support, Policy Making, and Participation in Governance. They point out that schools of library and information science are unlikely to ever show particularly well in terms of Centrality. Unless universities recognize the importance of course offerings in the location and use of modern information sources, and the schools move to provide these generally on a service basis, this is certainly correct. The library itself, on the other hand, can make a strong argument for centrality and, in fact, this will typically be its chief source of power.

Excellence will normally mean a high level of publication in refereed journals of high quality. One might presume that it means high quality instruction as well, but since real output measures of the effectiveness of instruction are not readily available, it normally does not. Most educational institutions consider a high level of instruction as a given, assuming a sufficient level of resources are available. Schools are certainly able to show well in the publication arena if they commit their efforts to doing so. Because of their size, however, this will require that comparisons are made to other schools of library and information science and that quantitative comparisons are normalized by faculty size. Gross publication rates can not be expected to compare well with much larger departments. A top ten English department is competing with thousands of other departments; a top ten school of library and information science has only sixty rivals. Academic libraries are much less likely to rely on output measures for reputations of excellence. Circulation is sometimes used, but reliance is more often on collection size and budget.

External support means grants, contracts, and development funds generated. Grants that bring overhead support to the institution are particularly prized. Libraries can certainly generate meaningful grant support and often receive gifts that are substantial. Since most of their alumni are not wealthy, and large corporate givers see little direct benefit from their support, schools of library and information science will not likely generate large endowments. There is certainly grant funding available for library and information science faculty who actively seek it, but not at the levels of the science and engineering departments to whom they might be compared.

Field support is important for schools of library and information science and for libraries. Both are heavily involved in local and national organizations, and the schools normally have large and vocal, if not wealthy, alumni. These organizations can offer real support in times of difficulty and often represent a meaningful power base. This base will not normally be apparent to academic administrators unless it is mobilized to address a specific issue.

Policy making implies advice to, and consultation with, governmental agencies. Heim and Ostertag find a low level of such participation in the library and information science community when compared with the effort in the field support area.[13] Participation in governance is another area of strikingly low involvement. A library and information science faculty may be able to do very little to improve centrality, and excellence and external support can only be strengthened relative to other similar schools. Participation in institutional governance, however, is certainly something that faculty can do in order to strengthen a school's power base. The personal contacts developed in this process can still make a very real difference on the margin in resource allocation processes. In a practical sense institutional service can have real importance in the academic environment. Generally, however, this applies only to institutional service outside the unit.

SERVICE TO THE SCHOOL

Faculty governance work within the school of library and information science has very little benefit in terms of supplementing the school's power base. This is so simply because it does not involve institutional contacts outside the school to any great extent. It is, however, the backbone of the academic structure, and what makes faculty employment unique.

The academic department is a remarkably stable structure, even though one can argue that it has not been appropriate for the differentiation of function that is currently required in academia.[14] There is no real administrative hierarchy in an academic unit on the department level. The chief administrator of a school of library and information science, whether the title is dean, director, or department chair, is normally, with two or three exceptions, operating at this stage. An organization chart would show the chief administrator and then everyone else. While the administrator may set the tone of the operation, and has some influence through budget control and faculty evaluations, the academic policies of the unit are set by the faculty through its committee structure. Such an administrator is at best a "first among equals," whose role is to apply the policy decisions set by the faculty on a daily basis, to provide an interface with the institution's higher administration, and to provide the resources that allow the faculty to carry out their academic duties.

In schools of library and information science small size normally guarantees that all faculty have the opportunity and obligation to participate directly in faculty governance at the school level. They normally do so, since not participating would be giving up a measure of direct control over their own daily working conditions. Internal school service is part of the daily life of most faculty and is viewed as part of a normal workload. Such service is generally expected from, and provided by, every faculty member. The absence of such service would be frowned on by deans and promotion committees, but its presence does not add any great value to a resume. The same can be said for student advising, which might be considered either teaching or service. Except for particularly meritorious service within the department, positive evaluation for service comes from public service and service in the academy, but external to the department.

SERVICE TO THE UNIVERSITY

Institutional service outside the department will involve much of the same governance activity as takes place at the department level. There will be regular committees at the college and university level on curriculum, promotion and tenure, and all the other committee functions that occur within the department. There will be additional committees that are concerned with such university-wide functions as the production of the academic calendar and the awarding of honors. Normally, bodies such as faculty councils or senates provide a faculty voice in university-wide policy matters and provide an opportunity for visible institutional service. Service as minor professors or outside examiners on doctoral committees may also have a salubrious effect.

It is also the case that the university may take advantage of the proficiency of its faculty for advice and consultation in planning its own activities, where another organization with less expertise available internally might well have to resort to external consultation. Faculty may also be utilized on selection committees to identify candidates for administrative and professional positions within the University. Such service increases visibility of the faculty and the school of library and information science and develops contacts that may be useful for collaboration and for the building of the power base.

WHO SHOULD SERVE?

One may well conclude that all academic faculty should accept a service component as part of their job description. There are clear benefits to the individual, the academic unit, the discipline or profession, and to the parent academic organization in their doing so. In the case of librarians and library and information science faculty, certain elements of the service component have received emphasis in the past. Service at the department level and service in professional organizations has been the norm. Institutional service outside the department has received a far smaller emphasis.

Service internal to the department will normally be required at some level, even if it is only student advising. It seems likely that even the most junior faculty members should be quickly involved in departmental faculty governance activities so that they can become acclimatized to that role. Since promotion and retention are likely to depend more heavily upon their teaching and research activities, requirements for institutional service outside the department should be light if they exist at all. Some limited form of service in a professional association would normally be expected as well.

Associate professors should most likely be expected to devote more time to institutional service outside the department, and to move into leadership roles in state and national organizations. Senior professors have some obligation to be known to their campus colleagues and to participate in campus wide governance to at least a limited extent.

It seems likely that deans and directors should encourage institutional service outside the department since there are benefits to the unit in such service in that it counters the isolation from other faculty that is often cited as a problem area. Such encouragement will likely mean that faculty evaluation will include a service component.

EVALUATING SERVICE ACTIVITY

How can service be evaluated? What is evaluated will naturally enough depend upon what is expected by an institution. Service at every level of the institution, department, college, and university, and at every level of community service, local, state, regional, national and international, might be required, or perhaps only departmental governance activities will be specified. At any rate, the level and extent of service expectations should be made clear at the outset, and standard rating forms should be utilized. Seldin provides a sample form and suggests that the following points be considered for institutional service.

Committee Work
Does the instructor attend regularly? Contribute actively to the work of the group? Are committee assignments accepted willingly? Is the committee better because of the instructor's participation? Do the other committee members share this appraisal?

Committee Chair
Is this person an effective chair? Are meetings called only for a specific purpose? Does the chair make appropriate use of each committee member's special expertise? Are passive members encouraged and aggressive members restrained? How skillfully? Has the chair arranged for committee minutes to be taken? Is needed material distributed to members to be read and considered in advance of the meeting?

Attitude Toward Institutional Service
Does the instructor willingly execute assignments? Volunteer to take on service tasks? How responsive is the instructor to the needs of the department? The institution?

General
How do you rate the instructor's service against others in the department? In the institution? What is needed to improve

the quality of that contribution (workshops or training seminars)?[15]

Public service is more likely to be judged by offices and chairs held in external organizations and by awards received from these organizations than it is by any rating of performance or attitude, since these will not normally be observable within the institution. The presence of ongoing consulting activity is in itself evidence of successful public service, since such activity is market-driven and, at least in the long run, will continue only when it provides value.

CONCLUSIONS

The faculty service role in academia is an important one, and is perhaps more important to librarians and the faculties of schools of library and information science than it may be to others. There are advantages to deans, directors, and personnel committees in seeing that such activities are well defined, clearly made part of the mission of those they must evaluate, and visibly incorporated into the evaluation instruments in use. This is not to say that service should be an equal component for evaluation with teaching and research. Very few in academia would support such a position. Service may be viewed as closely tied with research and with faculty development activity, and can be pursued with these ends in mind. It has its own benefits separate from these, however.

Service is no more or less difficult to objectively evaluate than teaching or research. The type and level of service activity desired will likely vary with a faculty member's seniority and proclivities. This may imply a certain minimum level of activity, with objectives for a higher level of activity set between the faculty member and the evaluator.

Librarians and faculties of schools of library and information science normally stress public service and departmental level institutional service. A change in emphasis toward broader institutional service could be of real assistance in supplementing their power bases within the academic environment.

NOTES

1. David D. Dill, "Research as a Scholarly Activity: Context and Culture," in *Measuring Faculty Research Performance*, ed. John W. Creswell (San Francisco: Jossey-Bass Inc., 1986), 11.

2. Pauline Wilson, "Factors Effecting Research Productivity," *Journal of Education for Librarianship* 20 (Summer 1979): 13.

3. Kathleen M. Heim, "Dimensions of Faculty Public Service: A Policy Science Approach to Questions of Information Provision, *Journal of Education for Library and Information Science* 26 (Winter 1986): 154-164.

4. Elizabeth Futas, "Faculty Role in Professional Associations: An Answer to Kathleen M. Heim's 'Dimensions of Faculty Public Service: A Policy Science Approach to Questions of Information Provision'," *Journal of Education for Library and Information Science* 27 (Winter 1986): 210-215.

5. Lionel S. Lewis, *Scaling the Ivory Tower: Merit and Its Limits in Academic Careers*, (Baltimore: Johns Hopkins University Press, 1975), 194.

6. Karen F. Smith et al., "Tenured Librarians in Large University Libraries," *College and Research Libraries* 45 (March 1984): 95.

7. Mary Kingsbury, "How Library Schools Evaluate Faculty Performance," *Journal of Education for Librarianship* 22 (Spring 1982): 236.

8. James L. Bess, *University Organization: A Matrix Analysis of the Academic Professions* (New York: Human Sciences Press, 1982), 157.

9. Peter Seldin, *Changing Practices in Faculty Evaluation: A Critical Assessment and Recommendations for Improvement* (San Francisco: Jossey-Bass Inc., 1984), 37.

10. Marion Paris, *Library School Closings: Four Case Studies* (Metuchen, NJ: Scarecrow Press, 1988), 149.

11. Lynn E. Gamble, "University Service: New Implications for Academic Librarians," *The Journal for Academic Librarianship* 14 (January 1989): 344-347.

12. Kathleen M. Heim and J. Keith Ostertag, "Sources of Institutional Power: An Analysis of Faculty Policy Participation as an Agent of Influence and Domain," *Library Quarterly* 61 (July 1991): 282-291.

13. Ibid., 288.
14. Bess, 64.
15. Seldin, 150.

Part III:
The Impact and Value of Teaching

*T*eaching is perhaps the greatest professional service of all, in which the teacher shares professional knowledge, life experiences, and perceptions with students, not for his or her own benefit, but for theirs. The act of instruction demands much of the teacher, and the rewards are frequently delayed, indirect, and intangible. Dr. Patterson's devotion to teaching is well-known to his past and present students and to his colleagues. All three of the faculty responsibility triumvirate of instruction, scholarship, and service are important but, of the three, teaching is most essential to the profession, for scholarship is empty if its results are not communicated through teaching, and teaching is indeed the utmost service. Through good teaching, the faculty member instills in students the need to perpetuate the instructional, scholarly, and service roles of the profession.

Connie Van Fleet explores the roles and responsibilities of the teacher as advisor and mentor in Chapter 7. In Chapter 8, Donald E. Riggs provides meaning and support for Dr. Patterson's insistence on the importance of "being a damn good librarian."

Chapter 7

ADVISING AND MENTORING: COMPLEMENTARY AND ESSENTIAL ROLES

Connie Van Fleet

Library administrators and educators have in recent years become interested in the phenomenon of mentoring. As concerns about the future of libraries and the profession grow, many responsible librarians have begun to explore mechanisms for recruiting and developing the next generation of leaders. Mentoring appears to be a natural and effective process that furthers the careers of those who demonstrate promise, and several articles have been written describing the responsibilities, benefits, and formal implementation of mentor/protege relationships in librarianship.[1]

Many authors, however, appear to view mentoring as a tool for advancing careers or developing leaders rather than as a highly personalized, individual relationship. This bias is reflective of the business management literature and overlooks the models and concerns of other disciplines which have explored mentoring relationships. To fully understand the implications of the term "mentoring" and to assess the feasibility of formal mentoring programs, it is important to recognize variations in basic approaches to the process. In addition, it should be recognized that the formal advising role offers a parallel, and sometimes more appropriate, model for those who wish to develop junior members of a profession.

ADVISORS AND MENTORS

Advising and mentoring are similar, yet distinct, functions. Advisors and mentors provide information about basic skills and requirements, knowledge about bureaucratic structures, and support during emotional or psychological difficulties. They act as guides for those who are less experienced in a given area, and even established leaders in a field seem to prefer this type of personal and person-embodied information.[2] Ideally, both advisors and mentors work on the basis of andragogical assumptions, respecting the talents and individuality of the dependent members of the relationship and guiding them along a continuum towards independence.

Nevertheless, there are very pronounced differences in the two types of relationships. The differences between advising and mentoring focus on duration, level and nature of involvement, degree of personal risk or investment, and intended outcomes. While one may attempt to provide clear delineations of the two roles, common (and sometimes exploitative) use of the term "mentor" has led to ambiguity in definition and the growth of varying conceptual models.

ADVISORS -- BASIC ROLES AND CHARACTERISTICS

An advisor is one who gives advice, judgment, or counsel to another, whether superior, junior, or equal in status. Although there are many instances of professionals acting in an advisory manner within an organization, the role that most closely approximates the mentoring relationship is found in the academic advisor model, which recognizes the unequal status of the two members.

The academic advisor, usually a faculty member and presumably then the more experienced and knowledgeable member of the academic community, clearly enjoys higher status than the advisee. The academic advisor position is generally institutionalized, and this role is often articulated as part of a faculty member's duties, although sometimes the expectation is implicit. The effective faculty advisor is knowledgeable, about both his or her own discipline and the organizational structure of the department and university. Because it is incumbent upon the advisor to deal with a number of students, not just a chosen few, he or she must be accepting of a wide variety of skill levels, personalities, goals, and priorities. Above all, the advisor must be honest and ethical, respecting students' privacy and needs while objectively ensuring equitable treatment for all students and adherence to university and departmental standards.

While the advisor may serve a number of functions in different realms of the students' lives -- informing them of regulations, guiding them through a course of study, or offering emotional or psychological support -- the limitations of the relationship are generally understood and typically endure only during the students' tenure in an academic program. That is, the relationship lasts as long as both the faculty advisor and the student are functioning within the same organization and attempting to meet the same specific, immediate goal. The investment on both sides, in terms of degree of involvement, personal identification, time, and ego, is minimal and risk is fairly negligible.

The advising model offers a number of advantages to the advisee, advisor, institution, and the profession. As indicated above, the advisee may expect help in dealing with bureaucratic structures, may expect guidance in developing an academic and professional career, and may expect in some measure to be protected from the consequences of inexperience or ignorance. Because the system is institutionalized, each student is assured of an advisor and equal access to the benefits an advisor/advisee relationship can offer. Advisors contribute to their own career advancement by fulfilling this obligation, enjoy the satisfaction of developing students, and share in the enhanced organizational stability and harmony resulting from students who have been informed of expectations and regulations and socialized into the system. The department and university benefit from this socialization of students and from having faculty assume responsibility for a somewhat bureaucratic function, not only saving some administrative costs and coopting faculty into sharing a bureaucratic view, but in fulfilling the organization's mission by enhancing the student's educational experience. And, ultimately, the profession will benefit from this one-on-one advising. All potential members of the profession can be recipients of a basic level of guidance at this entry level. Each should receive advice and counsel that will help him or her develop individual talents and skills in a way that will ultimately benefit not only a personal career, but a profession. Finally, this type of formalized advising program provides the type of atmosphere conducive to the growth of the deeper and more longlasting mentoring relationship.

The advisor model offers clear and appropriate guidelines for formalized staff development programs, particularly inasmuch as the primary impetus is the benefit to the organization and the focus is on advancement within the specific institution. While effective fulfillment of advising responsibilities may depend on an institutionalized structure that encourages opportunity and guidance for all junior members, the mentoring relationship, which involves a much greater level of involvement and personal risk, remains a serendipitous occurrence that can be fostered, but not dictated. It is likely that the mentoring relationship is valued so highly simply because it involves so few. While advising is available to all, a mentor will select as proteges only those who have in some way demonstrated exceptional promise.

RECURRING INTEREST IN MENTORSHIP

There are a number of reasons that mentoring has become a topic of recurring interest. As women become more career-oriented, they feel that they are not beneficiaries of the same type of relationships ("the old boy network") that their male counterparts seem to form. Beyond this female-oriented side of the issue, both men and women have found that upward mobility is more difficult than in previous decades and that security in the organizational environment is a concept that became obsolete in the 1960's.

Zey ascribes the interest in mentoring to "the demographic realities of our time."[3] Among these he includes the large number of well-educated peers vying for jobs, the shrinking ranks of middle management, acquisitions and merger practices that eliminate positions and give no points for loyalty or experience, and recessionary conditions that limit growth and expansion. Additionally, a number of studies have demonstrated the seeming efficacy of mentoring as a career strategy.[4] In essence, developing a mentoring relationship can give an ambitious young person a competitive edge. Although some studies have suggested that mentoring is a fairly common phenomenon in the corporate world, and young executives have been led to believe that it is essential that they seek out and attach themselves to mentors, Zey finds the rarity of mentoring relationships "striking."[5]

In librarianship, we have seen a continuous emphasis on staff development and personnel training. Given that personnel expenditures continue to account for the largest line in most library budgets, this is hardly surprising. In addition, faced with changing conditions and poorly articulated goals, the profession has given more thought to the necessity of developing quality leaders who can guide libraries through the challenges that lie ahead. A rather natural meeting point for these two trends is an exploration of mentoring processes and programs as a mechanism for identifying and grooming new leaders for librarianship. Perhaps, too, as librarians become more aware of private sector practices and adopt more strategies from the corporate world (for example, quantitative evaluation, accountability measures, marketing), it is natural that they would follow on the heels of business in its renewed interest in mentoring.

Librarians will find it necessary to adapt these programs, and perhaps even the underlying conceptual models that drive them in order to accommodate the different intended outcomes. While the corporate sector develops mentoring programs to strengthen individual organizations and mentors and proteges participate in them to develop personal careers, the library profession is attempting to develop a new generation who can think beyond personal ambition and localized institutions to lead the profession with enthusiasm and vision.

MENTORS -- DEFINITIONS

Zey, in his study of the mentoring phenomenon in the corporate world, defines a mentor as "a person who *oversees* the career and development of another person, usually a junior, through teaching, counseling, providing psychological support, protecting, and at times promoting or sponsoring."[6] This definition suggests the level and intensity of a mentoring relationships.

Carrying this idea even further is the response of this would-be protege, who expects that a mentor will be someone who:

> acts as a coach, much like in athletics, advising and teaching the political nuts and bolts, giving feedback, and rehearsing strategies. He or she provides you with exposure, visibility, and sponsorship, helping open doors to promotions and seeing that you get assignments that will get you noticed. And mentors take the blame for your mistakes, acting as protectors until you're established enough to shoulder criticism on your own.[7]

The relationship has benefits for the institution and mentor as well, and it is not surprising that interest in mentorship has grown over the past several years. Yet these definitions merely hint at the underlying philosophies that may affect the use of the term "mentoring" and the subsequent attempts to encourage or formalize the process.

TRADITIONAL CONCEPTUAL FRAMEWORKS OF MENTORSHIP

A study of the literature suggests that there are two basic conceptual frameworks used in developing models of the grooming-mentoring relationship in which a senior partner (mentor) develops and protects a junior member. This division stems from the work of Marcel Mauss, whose anthropological studies identified two separate systems of economy within social groups, the market economy system and the gift exchange system. The "market economy" model generally serves as the mentorship model for the corporate sector, while professions such as education and counseling emphasize the human relationship and personal, rather than career, benefits usually associated with "gift exchange" theory.[8]

Much of the language employed in the library literature seems to parallel the "market economy" model. Perhaps libraries have adopted the market economy rather than gift exchange because we have come to view information as a commodity and patrons as clients or customers. Perhaps it is because we have become increasingly dependent on the corporate sector for short-term solutions. It may be that we have adopted and transformed these models without articulating the differences in our underlying vision. The models have a certain degree of commonality, and the motivation and ultimate visions that distinguish them may not always be readily apparent.

The Market Economy Model

The market economy model is not identified as such by those who follow it. The corporate view of mentoring does not deal in philosophical issues to a great degree. It is a strategy to be employed for career progression and organizational effectiveness. Zey suggests that the mentoring process is part of the "shadow organization" in business, the informal structure that parallels the visible, articulated one.[9]

In the corporate sector, the organization condones, even encourages mentoring, as a means of socializing new members and quickly developing top managers. Organizational communication is enhanced, managerial successions are smoothed, and productivity is increased.[10] The protege receives knowledge, enhanced growth, protection, and rapid career advancement. The mentor is rewarded by increased status (being seen as someone who can spot talent), a reputation for efficiency (getting the job done through delegation), and an enhanced power base (built on the loyalty of proteges).[11] In addition, the protege contributes to the mentor's communication network, providing intelligence or information and sometimes acting in an advisory role. Although some mentors or proteges may be driven by altruistic motives, "at root the mentor relationship exists and thrives only to the extent that the participants expect their careers to be positively affected by it."[12]

Some aspects of the market economy mentoring model, as evidenced in recent literature, appear to be a corruption of the traditional mentoring model, which develops over an extended period through personal interest and affection and has mutual respect and loyalty as primary characteristics. Now, young executives are exhorted to seek out a mentor, choosing carefully, weighing such factors as the mentor's power base and connections, and to consider developing multiple mentors to reduce personal risk in the event that a mentor is displaced.[13] Nevertheless, when both mentor and protege work from the same expectations, it appears that the mentoring relationship works effectively in the corporate sector.

The mentor performs a number of roles: teaching, personal support, organizational intervention, and promotion. These four roles represent a continuum in which the mentor's investment changes in nature and in which the risk increases.[14] In teaching, level I in the hierarchy proposed by Zey, the primary investment is time. The mentor teaches the job by providing instruction in skills, explaining the organizational structure and politics, and outlining career options.[15] At the second level, the mentor begins to risk emotional involvement and offers a more personal relationship, providing psychological support through times of transition and stress, confidence building, and assistance with personal concerns.[16] If the relationship advances, the mentor will begin to offer organizational support, protecting the candidate in times of conflict or upheaval, marketing the candidate, and providing access to resources that would not normally be available to a junior person.[17] At this point, the mentor/protege relationship becomes much more public, and the mentor is now risking organizational relationships and his or her own reputation. Finally, at the level of greatest involvement, the mentor risks his or her own reputation and career by sponsoring the protege, that is, either promoting or arranging for the promotion of the protege.[18]

The mentoring relationship has been found to pass through a number of phases, and the transitions seem to be particularly difficult times.[19] Beginning with the initiation phase, in which mentor and protege first begin to recognize the possibilities of a close relationship, the process continues through a cultivation phase, in which the relationship becomes deeper and the goal of advancing the protege's career is realized. The separation phase, in which the relationship is terminated because it has ceased to serve the original purpose, either through a change in circumstances or the growth of the protege, is particularly difficult. In successful relationships, however, the process continues through a fourth and final phase of redefinition, in which each partner can respect the other and the new relationship. Kram compares the course of the mentoring relationship to that of a love affair, which, if gotten through successfully, ends as a friendship between peers.[20]

The mentoring relationship is, of course, not without risk. The mentor spends a great deal of time and energy that might be better spent on business. In addition, mentoring at the higher levels involves exposure of the self -- both the ego and the corporate self. Choice of an incompetent or disloyal protege can reflect negatively on the mentor.[21] The protege risks attracting the envy of peers who have not been singled out and becoming embroiled in office politics. He or she may become overly dependent on the mentor, either in actuality or psychologically, doubting his or her own achievements and abilities. Additionally, a protege who has become closely identified with a mentor may find himself in a difficult position should the mentor change organizations, either willingly or unwillingly.[22] The organization may find itself distracted from the business at hand through political infighting and circumvention of carefully developed structures for promotion and advancement.

The opportunity for negative, as well as positive, results is characteristic of virtually all mentorship models. The market economy model works well in the corporate sector where all parties are driven by the same goals and understand the fundamental nature of the relationship. Alternative models of the mentoring process have been recognized by scholars in other disciplines, however, and should be explored for their potential value to the library and information science profession.

The Gift Exchange Concept

The "gift exchange" concept has been proposed by humanists as an alternative and "truer" model of mentoring than that promoted in corporate circles in the language of business. Gehrke underlines the differences in vocabulary and, ultimately, perspective.

> The metaphors that predominate in our speech about relationships and events shape our thinking and behavior . . . The use of market metaphors obfuscates the nature of the mentor-protege phenomenon. It can lead to a confusion between the real gift exchange relationship and such marketplace phenomena as patronage and sponsorship.[23]

In the "gift exchange" conceptual framework, then, the giver and receiver are bound by rules that transcend exchange of career-oriented benefits. To qualify as a gift exchange, the process must meet certain rather stringently defined criteria, and both giver and receiver are obligated to work within the framework. Gehrke delineates four conditions that must occur within the exchange:

   1. The gift must be created by the person who will be the giver, that is, the mentor. The wisdom, stature, or

power that the mentor has developed over a lifetime and as part of his or her own career becomes the creation that is shared. The new vision that the protege develops is the priceless gift.

2. The gift must cause a transformation in the receiver. Most often, this transformation involves not only a new way of looking at the world, but of perceiving oneself -- a growing confidence and belief in one's own abilities.

3. The exchange is sustained (advanced) by the recipients commitment to labor as a means of demonstrating worthiness. In humanistic circles, this encompasses the work of redefining self, not just one's career.

4. And finally, essentially, the gift must be passed on to a new recipient. The protege becomes mentor, giving the gift of the original mentor's wisdom, now enhanced by his or her own experience and wisdom.[24]

This "gift exchange" theory of mentoring assures the same type of continuity that we saw as a benefit of the market economy approach, yet on a wider scale. While those who study corporate mentoring talk about continuity within the organization, those who discuss mentoring as a gift exchange seem to have a broader view of the nature and value of this grounding in the past and focus toward the future. It is not just the organization that benefits, but the profession and society. Yet at the same time, the responsibility is a keenly felt personal obligation. "The passage of the gift binds people to each other. It therefore becomes a vehicle of cohesiveness in the culture."[25] A number of examples of the continuity and impetus offered by a mentoring relationship are apparent in librarianship. In *Resources in History: An Introductory Guide*, Fritze, Coutts, and Vyhnanek acknowledged their gratitude to Charles Patterson, a respected faculty member and dedicated reviewer with whom they had studied.[26]

The benefits to the individuals involved in a mentoring relationship based on gift exchange are parallel to those provided by the commodity exchange relationships: knowledge, prestige, and power, as are the risks attendant in a public personal relationship. The emphasis, however, is in the relationship itself, rather than in career progression or recognition, although these may be expected outcomes.

COMMONALITIES OF GROOMING-MENTORING MODELS

One of the most outstanding characteristics of mentoring, regardless of model, is the reciprocity of the relationship. That is, both mentor and protege contribute to the process and both gain from the experience. Each partner, regardless of model, contributes to the exchange in terms of time, effort, loyalty, personal status, and ego, although the relative levels of involvement may vary depending on which conceptual framework one espouses.

Whether the protege is rewarded by rapid career growth in the corporate sector or new opportunities for self-actualization, it is clear that the more dependent partner benefits from the relationship. What has become equally apparent is that the mentor benefits as well, whether through status and support in the organization or through prestige and renewal on a personal basis. In one of the most dramatic findings to reinforce the benefits of the relationship to the mentor, Keele and DeLaMare-Schaefer concluded that being a mentor served to further a career as effectively as having been a protege. They found that the benefits one would expect to accrue to the protege also accrued to the mentor, including upward career mobility, control of the work environment, development of a support network, increased access to resources, enhanced status, and personal satisfaction.[27]

Additionally, an examination of risk indicates that this factor is present in all models of the process. No mentoring relationship is without risk for both partners. As delineated above, risk in the "market economy" model tends to focus on organizational factors: poor performance by either the mentor or protege, shifts in the power structure, or accusations of favoritism all present very real risks.[28] While these may be risks in the "gift exchange" model as well, the major risks perceived tend to involve personal and egoistic problems.[29]

In sum, grooming-mentoring relationships are distinguished from advising relationships by their comprehensiveness (not confined to one aspect or dimension of life) and mutuality, as well as informality, intense level of interaction, and time of endurance.[30]

Networking-Mentoring

A fairly recent form of mentoring that is gaining popularity is the networking-mentoring model, which is seen as an alternative to the more traditional grooming-mentoring models discussed above. Those grooming-mentoring models, whether based on the market economy or gift exchange concept, have several weaknesses: they tend to be homogeneous, because mentors choose proteges who are similar to themselves; they are based on favoritism, because mentors are committed to the interests of their proteges over the interests of others; and they are characterized by intense relationships, because of the depth and scope of interaction. These weaknesses may lead to strong conflict and emotional confrontation, the exclusion of groups who are new to professional positions, and waste of valuable personnel resources.[31]

Swoboda and Millar suggest networking-mentoring as a more appropriate process for professional women. This process involves "flexible and mutually interdependent patterns of training, information sharing, and support."[32] The relationship is in a constant state of change, and characterized by equality and peer interaction, rather than a hierarchical relationship. While this form of mentoring enhances career development, it does not move the participants up the ladder as quickly as a positive grooming-mentoring relationship. It does, however, have the advantage of being open to all and results in greater self-reliance, less resentment from colleagues, and freedom from the risk of a mentor/protege relationship turned sour.[33]

CONCLUSION

Although there is a great deal of commonality in the general structure of mentoring relationships, the choice of conceptual model determines the motives, roles, progress and, indeed, expected outcome of the process. Perhaps the most important conclusion of this discussion is that people will often have different expectations from mentoring relationships. While all parties may recognize the basic structure, the conceptual frameworks and resulting goals and outward phenomena each anticipates may be very different. If the relationship is to remain positive, it is essential that partners share a common vision.

While much of the literature has dealt with formalized, institutionalized "mentoring" programs, these might more aptly be described as advising programs. The guidelines for an advising model can easily be incorporated into an organization's staff development program. The academic advisor serves as the role model for the established or senior partner in these formal programs. The professor as advisor interacts objectively with many students, providing basic guidance, bureaucratic expertise, and emotional support. This is an integral part of a faculty member's responsibilities, and the university supports this role by providing time and recognition. An organization that hopes to implement a successful advising program will find it necessary to provide similar resources and incentives.

True mentoring is much more difficult to institutionalize. Yamamoto, in exploring formalized mentoring programs developed for career advancement asserts that

> mentoring has come to mean in many quarters little more than . . . assistance in social

networking, coaching for professional skills, or apprenticeship for career advancement. In such a context, we must acknowledge that yet another human phenomenon of profundity is being threatened by a misguided attempt at popularization and standardization.[34]

Some who have been involved in formal business-mentor programs suggest that such a program is not simply a diluted version of a true mentor relationship. "It's a perversion of it. . . . The mentor can't get interested in knowing what my dreams are, unless my dreams are advancing the company. I can't tell him if I'm not sure I want to keep working for this terrible company. How can I, when he's there to make me more promotable?"[35]

Many corporations have found that those programs which most closely emulate spontaneous mentoring relationships are the most successful. Yet some authors argue that formal mentoring programs are based on a faulty premise. Hurley argues that

> The reciprocity required of any true mentor-protege relationship -- the mutual respect and liking, the mutual choosing, the mutual give-and-take -- puts into doubt the fundamental assumption of most formal mentor programs that a mentor is like a pill that can be administered to a protege once a week, for a few hours, with guaranteed results.[36]

It appears that an organization can, at best, provide an atmosphere that is conducive to the open, trusting, and interactive exchanges that are the basis of mentoring relationships.

Yet while these relationships are difficult to institutionalize, they are perhaps not so much essential as inevitable. The reciprocal benefits of the relationship, structures of professions, and the nature of the human psyche seem to work together to ensure that rare and serendipitous joining of the wise advisor and the beloved student.

Both formalized advising structures and mentoring relationships exist in the academic environment, and the integration and recognition of these parallel models works very well. It is admirable that librarians are seeking new ways in which to develop the leaders so vital to our profession. Perhaps the recognition of a dual system will allow us to formulate the very best formalized programs we can provide, while allowing us the scope and inspiration to develop true mentoring relationships that will benefit our profession as well as our careers and institutions.

NOTES

1. See, for example, Cargill's excellent overview in Jennifer Cargill, "Developing Library Leaders: The Role of Mentorship," *Library Administration & Management* 3 (Winter 1989): 12-15 or Elfreda Chatman's penetrating study, "The Role of Mentorship in Shaping Public Library Leaders," *Library Trends* 40 (Winter 1992): 492-512. Other articles of interest include Davis S. Ferriero, "ARL Directors as Proteges and Mentors," *The Journal of Academic Librarianship* 7 (January 1982): 358-265 and Sue S. Stalcup, "Mentoring: A Tool for Career Enhancement," *Library Personnel News* 3 (Winter 1989): 4-5.

2. Connie Van Fleet and Joan Durrance, "Public Library Leaders and Research: Mechanisms, Perceptions, and Strategies," *Journal of Education for Library and Information Science* 34 (Spring 1993): in press.

3. Michael Zey, *The Mentor Connection* (Homewood, IL: Dow-Jones-Irwin, 1984), 4-6.

4. Elfreda Chatman, "The Role of Mentorship;" Caela Farren, Janet Dreyfus Gray and Beverly Kaye, "Mentoring: A Boon to Career Development," *Personnel* 61, no. 6 (Nov.-Dec. 1984): 20-24; Kathy Kram, "Phases of the Mentor Relationship," *Academy of Management Journal* 26 (1983): 608-625.

5. The number of articles about mentoring in education, counseling, and business journals (as well as popular women's magazines) has escalated over the past decade, to the point of creating some anxiety for career people who have not had mentors. See, for instance, Marilyn Haring-Hidore, "Mentoring as a Career Enhancement Strategy for Women," *Journal of Counseling and Development* 66 (November 1987): 147-48; Reba L. Keele and Mary DeLaMare-Schaefer, "So What Do You Do Now That You Didn't Have a Mentor?" *Journal of the National Association of Women Deans, Administrators, and Counselors* 47, no.3 (1984): 36-40; Zey, 6.

6. Zey, 7.

Advising and Mentoring

7. C. McPartland, "The Myth of the Mentor," *Campus Voice* 2, no. 1 (1985): 8-11. Cited in Nathalie Gehrke, "Toward a Definition of Mentoring," *Theory Into Practice* 27 (Summer 1988): 190-94.

8. Gehrke, 191.

9. Zey, 1.

10. Ibid., 93.

11. Ibid., 78.

12. Ibid., 18.

13. John A. Byrne, "Let a Mentor Lead You -- But Beware the Pitfalls," *Business Week* (April 20, 1987): 95.

14. Zey, 14.

15. Ibid., 25-30.

16. Ibid., 35.

17. Ibid., 43.

18. Ibid., 51.

19. Kram, 621-623.

20. Ibid., 608-625.

21. Zey, 90.

22. Byrne, 95.

23. Gehrke, 193.

24. Ibid., 192.

25. Ibid., 191.

26. Ronald H. Fritze, Brian E. Coutts, and Louis A. Vyhnanek, *Reference Sources in History: An Introductory Guide* (Santa Barbara, CA: ABC-Clio, 1990), xvii.

27. Reba L. Keele and Mary DeLaMare-Schaefer, "So What Do You Do Now That You Didn't Have a Mentor?" *Journal of the National Association for Women Deans, Administrators, & Counselors* 47, no. 3 (Spring 1984): 36-40. Summarized in Martin Gerstein, "Mentoring: An Age Old Practice in a Knowledge-Based Society" *Journal of Counseling and Development* 64 (October 1985): 156-157.

28. Byrne, 95.

29. Kaoru Yamamoto, "To See Life Grow: the Meaning of Mentorship," *Theory Into Practice* 27 (Summer 1988): 185-188.

30. Beverly Hardcastle, "Spiritual Connections: Proteges' Reflections on Significant Mentorships," *Theory Into Practice* 27 (Summer 1988): 202.

31. Marion J. Swoboda and Susan B. Millar, "Networking-Mentoring: Career Strategy of Women in Academic Administration," *Journal of National*

Association of Women Deans, Administrators, and Counselors 49 (Fall 1986): 8-13.

32. Ibid., 11.

33. Haring-Hidore, 148.

34. Yamamoto, 188.

35. Daniel J. Levinson, *The Seasons of a Man's Life*, in Dan Hurley, "The Mentor Mystique," *Psychology Today* 22, no. 5 (May 1988): 43.

36. Hurley, 43.

Chapter 8

BEING A DAMN GOOD LIBRARIAN

Donald E. Riggs

Librarianship is one of our society's most honorable professions. It appeals to people who want to serve others. The profession attracts many who have tried other careers before deciding on librarianship (the average age of 1991 library and information science graduates was 34.5 years). Those who have engaged in library work, however, tend to remain in the field.

THE SERVICE PHILOSOPHY: CHARACTERISTICS OF LIBRARIANS AND LIBRARIANSHIP

Among other characteristics, a librarian demonstrates a high level of intelligence, an inquiring mind, a "love" for books and other carriers of information, a generalist and/or specialist background, and a strong desire to help others. Generally, persons entering the profession are not driven by materialism. Librarianship has been and is a low-paying profession; intrinsic values (other than money) attract and retain librarians.

Does librarianship have a theoretical base? In 1933, Butler stated:

> Unlike his colleagues in other fields of social activity the librarian is strangely uninterested in the theoretical aspects of the profession. He seems to possess a unique immunity to that curiosity which elsewhere drives modern man to attempt, somehow, an orientation of his particular labors with the main stream of human life. The librarian apparently stands alone in the simplicity of his profession: a rationalization of each immediate technical process by itself seems to satisfy his intellectual interest.[1]

A "theoretical base" is a mental construct. It is evident that librarianship has such a base. Librarianship, like medicine and music, has a body of generalizations and principles developed in association with practice in its field of activity and forming its content. It also encompasses a general frame of reference for inquiry (e.g., formulating hypotheses, undertaking action). As "information science" becomes more an integral part of "library science," we are witnessing the growth of a broader theoretical base.

Along with this intellectual base, a prudent beginning librarian develops a philosophy of service. It is surprising to see the reactions when veteran librarians are asked, "What is your philosophy of service?" How can one be a practicing librarian without some semblance of a philosophy of service? Perhaps one of the reasons for the puzzled expressions when librarians are asked to expound on their philosophy is that they have been too "busy" doing their assigned tasks to think about their philosophy.

With the freshly-minted M.L.S., the new librarian normally takes a position which matches his or her interests and educational background. The first job in one's chosen profession is very important, as early and lasting impressions are formed about the profession from the first work assignment. Too many times, beginning librarians are given the routine assignments (the donkey work, to paraphrase Peter Drucker). Supervisors often believe that the "baby" librarian needs experience at the ground level before being given any "intellectual" assignments. This is a mistake and it will force the beginning librarian to seek another position internally or go to another library. With the average age of the beginning librarian being in the mid 30s, supervisors should quickly involve their new colleagues in problem solving and other intellectual vigors of the library, and not lose or misuse this valuable human talent. First impressions of one's library assignment may be long lasting.

THE SERVICE PHILOSOPHY MADE MANIFEST: EFFECTIVE WORK HABITS

Like first impressions, the formulation of work habits is of major significance. Some libraries offer an environment for those who want to do enough to "just get by." That is, some librarians go to work each day and do only the bare minimum amount of work. These employees have retired early on the job; they do not "stretch" themselves. They believe the work they accomplish each day is all they should give to their library and profession. Why does such an attitude exist? Primarily, the answer is found in the work habits developed during the beginning librarian's first five years in the profession. In my twenty-seven years' experience (in school and academic libraries, and six years as a public library trustee), I have noticed several highly capable colleagues who do not "live up" to the expectations of others. These are not lazy individuals; they are mostly colleagues who essentially do not have good work habits.

Who is responsible for the development of work habits? The employee? The supervisor? Experience suggests that all parties concerned share this responsibility. The use of mentors for beginning librarians is now a common practice. The mentor, if qualified and motivated, can serve as a role model in the formulation and implementation of effective work habits. With the right mindset on the part of the beginning librarian, the supervisor, and the mentor, the creation of effective work habits should occur without too much difficulty. Some of the aspects of effective work habits include:

High Standards

Regardless of position in the library, one's performance should be geared toward the highest attainable standard. Anything less will eventually lead to mediocrity. Performance standards should be established, in most instances, so achievement can be measured in a quantifiable manner. Operating from the highest standard vantage will be one of the factors that will be necessary if one expects to be "a damn good librarian." One should not become overwhelmed with the standards issue, but it is essential to make it a regular ingredient of one's work habits.

Productivity

Strategies for measurement and enhancement of productivity depend on the specialty of the librarian. For example, catalogers can develop more efficient work habits, enabling them to increase the number of books cataloged each day. OCLC and RLG/RLIN have enabled catalogers to migrate from copy cataloging to original cataloging. The national utilities have made it possible for nonprofessionals to perform the copy cataloging functions, subsequently allowing librarians to raise their productivity in the area of original cataloging. The reference librarian can "work smarter" by developing skills for determining precisely what the user is seeking and getting the right information into the user's hands. Productivity has to be a concern of all library employees. Each can offer insight into how more work and greater results be achieved at less cost and a reduced expenditure of energy. More emphasis will be placed on how to take work out of the library's operations during the 1990s. The concept of total quality management fits nicely with the practice of reducing or eliminating unnecessary work while concurrently raising productivity. Librarians are strongly encouraged to develop methods that work effectively as well as efficiently. Library users must be kept in focus as the primary recipients of improved productivity.

Motivation

The literature of management is replete with generalizations about human motivation. Without the notion that something can motivate, instigate, or initiate change, one is left with a world of chance happening. In bringing about change, thinking moves automatically to motivational considerations: "I wonder why he said that?" "What should I do to get her to change her mind?" Motivational characteristics are difficult to pinpoint for individuals, although motivation is considered by many to be the key to behavior.

Almost every leading writer in the field has felt obligated to espouse some plan by which human actions can be understood and, therefore, controlled. If such observations on motivation are frightening to some, then a word of consolation is easily found. While various theories analyze methods of motivating people to do better work, and the manager will have an understanding of these theories, the very complexity of the human personality indicates that human motivation will never be subject to simple formulas.

Although motivation is to some extent the responsibility of library managers, it is a good habit for librarians to develop self-motivation techniques. A professional can rely only so much on external factors for motivation. Identifying annual goals and striving to achieve them is one way of motivating oneself. It is expected that different levels of motivation will be demonstrated by different librarians in pursuing any team or individual goal. The librarian's personal expectations regarding an endeavor's desired outcomes will likely temper enthusiasm. Nevertheless, the beginning professional should demonstrate a commitment to institutional goals and the willingness to act as a contributing member of the organization in achieving those goals.

Time Management; Setting Priorities

Time is one of the librarian's most precious commodities and judicious management of time is of signal importance. Learning how to manage one's time is an excellent habit. Disciplined focus is what distinguishes those librarians who make things happen from those who watch things happen. Following are some suggestions for improving the use of a librarian's time:

1. Identifying areas of the job with the greatest potential contribution to the library.
2. Developing goals for each critical success area.
3. Setting weekly priorities to facilitate the accomplishment of goals.
4. Doing the most important things first and never wasting time on unimportant activities.
5. Concentrating on a few things at a time.
6. Establishing deadlines.
7. Setting aside a few minutes each day to think about creative ways to improve the performance of the library department/area.
8. Avoiding unnecessary meetings.
9. Delegating.
10. Minimizing unproductive time for colleagues/staff.

Striving for clearly-defined short- and long-range goals is a necessity in effective time-management. These goals must be realistic and achievable. Nothing will destroy credibility faster than proposing to do things that one cannot accomplish. After identifying specific attainable goals and objectives, the librarian must not be dissuaded or distracted from achieving them.[2] Nearly all activities in which librarians are involved will be judged on the basis of their ultimate as well as their immediate value to the library. Special attention should be paid to Kipling's meaningful admonition to "fill every unforgiving minute with sixty seconds' worth of distance run," even though the results realized may be sometimes deferred.³ Placing emphasis on priorities has been with us for a long time, as reflected in the following verse:

> Let all things be done decently and in order.
> -- Corinthians, I, 14

The Extra Mile

The people in librarianship who make a difference, as in most other professions, are normally those who have a strong commitment to their field, and who are willing to expend extra effort and energy. The librarian who works only an eight-to-five day rarely leaves a mark on the library or the profession. This does not imply that these less committed individuals are not valuable colleagues: some are more efficient than others in their daily output. Activities that surpass minimal commitment are varied and encompass all facets of librarianship. Developing a new service program, revising an existing library instructional program, implementing a user self-sufficiency project, creating new techniques for preservation, holding a leadership position in a library organization/association, or writing an article or book on a new topic in the field are only samples of some ways to go "beyond the call of duty" in bettering one's library or contributing to the profession.

Librarianship offers many opportunities to make a difference; there is plenty of room for persons of high energy. It is a good habit to do more than is expected, even if it involves some personal inconvenience (e.g., occasionally working at night or on a weekend). Barbara Jordan, the first black congresswoman from Texas, best summarizes this concept, when she says, "Each day you have to look into the mirror and say to yourself, 'I'm going to be the best I can no matter what it takes.'"[4]

A Sense of Humor

Sometimes we are all guilty of taking ourselves too seriously. Libraries, like other human organizations, need to allow for humor and goodwill. With greater emphasis placed on the human component in the 1990s, we need to be able to laugh at ourselves and with our colleagues. Humanistic management of libraries is projected to make human interactions much smoother and more meaningful. A good laugh is excellent medicine for relieving stress and anxiety. Very few articles and books have been written on the importance of a sense of humor within organizations. Perhaps as organizations become more "human oriented," greater attention will be given to this most important ingredient.

The foregoing aspects of effective work habits are not inclusive; they merely represent a personal basis for effective action. These habits of work can be learned and practiced at any age, although it may be easier to form habits when one is young than to acquire them later. The good habits formed now will serve in good stead for the rest of a career. The good habits not formed now may never develop. Is it ever too late to learn new work habits? The answer is, "no." Longfellow said, "Nothing is too late, till the heart shall cease to palpitate."[5] The key is to start -- now.

THE SERVICE PHILOSOPHY MATURED: CONTINUED GROWTH

Continuing Education

It is becoming increasingly more important for the librarian to continue education and learning beyond the M.L.S. Since the ways things are done in libraries continue to change (e.g., AACR2, online public access catalogs), today's and tomorrow's librarians have little choice but to continue to learn. The librarian who chooses not to keep up with new developments will soon become obsolete. Continuing education is frequently equated with pursuing another degree. Studying for a second master's or the doctorate is a commendable venture, but the practical knowledge gained from these degrees may be dated in a few short years after receipt. True and meaningful continuing education will persist throughout one's working life, and possibly beyond.

Workshops and programs on appropriate topics tend to be the usual path in obtaining additional information or training. Libraries are beginning to redirect part of their budgets to continuing education and staff development. Typically, one per cent or less of a library's personnel budget is spent on continuing education or staff development activities. While for-profit organizations spend as much as three percent of their personnel budget for continuing education and staff development. Libraries should follow this example. No better investment can be made than in having an informed staff. The quality of library service offered will correlate with the up-to-date knowledge held by the staff.

Librarians have a unique environment in which to keep current with major events in their field. Since librarians have the skills to find new information in the literature, they are encouraged to engage in "self-imposed seminars." These "seminars" involve identifying an area or field of interest and then delving into the literature to learn more about the respective topic. For example, to learn more about the application of expert systems, the librarian could read selected books and journal articles on the topic. Perhaps an end product of this endeavor might be an article for a journal. Knowledge of interlibrary loan and resource sharing provides access to practically any journal article or book from anywhere in the world.

Such an approach to keeping oneself well informed does not cost much, and can be done at different times of the day and week. What is one of the most important ingredients in this type of continuing education? Self-motivation! One of the criticisms of this type of continuing education is that it does not work very well because it is left up to individual options and initiative, and it is true that self-discipline is essential for success in this type of independent research. Again, establishing priorities is important. Is it a greater benefit to attend an opera or to go to a ball game? One has to make these types of decisions.

Professional Activities

The number of professional meetings held annually by library-related organizations continues to expand significantly. There is little excuse for a librarian not to participate in some of these professional meetings. Local and state library associations offer some outstanding programs. Regional organizations do likewise. Resource sharing networks (e.g., AMIGOS, SOLINET) provide excellent training programs, and ALA holds as many as 2,500 meetings during its annual conference. As someone observed, "You tend to get out of a profession what you put into it." The "true" professional extends activities beyond the walls of the local library. Professional organizations offer opportunities not only to attend excellent continuing education and training programs, but to engage in the leadership of the respective organization. Holding an office in an organization is a superb way to develop leadership skills. Conducting a meeting builds confidence, and organizational skills can be fine-tuned by holding a committee to the agenda while achieving the desired outcomes of the meeting. Group dynamics learned in these meetings can improve effectiveness with groups in the local library.

Participation in library organizations allows the opportunity to become better acquainted with national colleagues in the same type of library work, and subsequently provides a broader base of colleagues to call upon when trying to solve problems in the individual's library. Librarians should not limit their professional involvement strictly to the library organizations and associations, however. A history subject specialist will find it appropriate to engage in activities of national historical associations. With greater use of computers in libraries, we are seeing more librarians participating in computing conferences (e.g., EDUCOM). Service on state, regional, and national committees usually are favorably recognized by the home base. Care should be taken not to get too involved with external committee work that may compete with primary work responsibility. Sometimes certain librarians are so effective on committees that they are asked by colleagues to take on more and more external committee assignments. A "tail wagging the dog" situation should be avoided. Professional activities, if properly tempered by a reasonable degree of participation, will undoubtedly improve a librarian's overall contribution to the local library.

THE SERVICE PHILOSOPHY ENGAGED: VISION AND LEADERSHIP

Creativity

One long-standing criticism of librarianship is the belief that librarians have very little opportunity to be creative. On the surface, such a belief may appear to be valid. When the user observes a librarian answering some reference questions, the assumption could be drawn that nearly anyone with an undergraduate education could do this type of work. Librarians can promote this type of assumption by actually engaging in work that does not require the M.L.S. Nevertheless, there is much room to use creative abilities in libraries.

The library's changing environment is setting the stage for greater creativity. Isaac Asimov puts creativity and the future in perspective:

> The work of the future will be creation, done by each in one's own fashion. People will judge you not by how long you work or how many routine units you turn out, but rather by how much you increase the joy of the world. They will want to know how much of what you do gives pleasure not only to yourself, but to others. How much is useful? That is what will count.[6]

The sometimes negative public image of the librarian may be reinforced by the routine work we often perform out of necessity. Observations of these routine activities help draw perceptions that being a librarian is dull, boring work. Nothing can be further from the truth. We librarians know the truth, but how do we demonstrate that our profession is fertile ground for new, creative endeavors?

Generally speaking, is creativity in libraries stifled or is it encouraged? The fact that libraries are arranged in a bureaucratic, systematic manner might lead one to believe that we have developed barriers that discourage creativity, yet nurturing creativity is the responsibility of all librarians, regardless of their respective positions in the library. Effective librarians do not wait until supervisors suggest employing more creativity in approaching the procedures and processes of daily work. Euster points out that creativity can be approached from various perspectives:

> Ways of looking at things from a different point of view.
> Ways to generate wide-ranging ideas.
> Ways to see new connections between problems and ideas previously thought to be unrelated.
> Ways to evaluate and understand one's own problem solving and creativity styles and strengths and weaknesses in these areas.[7]

Schools of library and information science can teach creativity, supervisors can encourage innovativeness, and organizations may offer creativity workshops, but the final burden of creativity lies with the professional. Kruger states this belief well:

> In order for librarians to continue developing as effective professionals, they must retain their spirit of adventure about the world, practice the profession in the spirit of celebration, and cultivate their own potential for creativity.[8]

Risk-Taking

> "What we need around here is more mistakes, not fewer!"
> -- Anonymous Library Manager

Similar to the encouragement of creativity in libraries is the need for more risk-takers. Library leaders carry the responsibility for creating a climate that fosters "calculated risk-taking." It would be simply foolish to take unwise risks that would jeopardize the library's basic functions. Risk-taking is not encouraged purely for the sake of such, but as a way of enhancing library services. Libraries are proven organizations in our society's fabric; they give valuable service and they have much credibility because they work.

There is no scientific approach that can be used in deciding which risks to take. The focus of risk-taking should be on maximizing opportunities rather than on minimizing risk. The parameters imposed on a library by its parent institution (e.g., university, city government) will inhibit some risk-taking. A balance must be struck between the immediate and easy opportunities for improvement and the long-range and difficult opportunities for innovation or changing the nature of the library. Drucker believes that the degree of risk is regarded as small or big not just on the basis on magnitude alone, but in consideration of its structure. He suggests that there are essentially four kinds of risk:

1. The risk one must accept; the risk that is built into the nature of the organization.
2. The risk one can afford to take.

3. The risk one cannot afford to take.
4. The risk one cannot afford not to take.[9]

Management and Leadership

Greater emphasis is now being placed on leadership in librarianship. The literature on the topic remains sparse. Librarians should strive to be both good managers and effective leaders. There is a difference between the two. Managers tend to work within defined bounds of known quantities, using well-established techniques to accomplish predetermined ends; the manager stresses means and how to achieve them. The leader focuses on the mission and how the library can effectively realize it. Managers focus on doing things right, while leaders place more value on doing the right things. Managers like to be efficient, while leaders like to be effective.

Libraries of all types need both efficient managers and effective leaders. Although some mistakenly perceive the director as the only manager in the library construct, leaders also exist in the library outside of the director's office. For example, the head of the interlibrary loan department may be a leader in the local library as well on the national level.

The trick is to appreciate and practice both management and leadership in libraries. Management is vital. Strong, dynamic leadership is absolutely necessary if libraries are to continue to effectively serve their constituents' information and research needs. Schools of library and information science must begin offering more courses on leadership, and planners of library conferences must schedule more programs on leadership. Schools of library and information science were offering courses on "administration" when business schools were teaching "management" courses; now business schools are teaching "leadership" while schools of library and information science are teaching "management." Perhaps some day soon we will catch up with our business colleagues. Bennis presents some interesting insights of leadership:

1. Leaders must develop the vision and strength to call the shots. There are risks in taking the initiative. The greater risk is to wait for orders.
2. The leader must be a "conceptualist" (not just someone to tinker with the "nuts and bolts").
3. The leader must have a sense of continuity and significance.
4. The leader must get at the truth and learn how to filter the unwieldy flow of information into coherent patterns. The biggest challenge of a leader -- any leader -- is getting the truth.
5. The leader must be a social architect who studies and shapes what is called the "culture of work" -- those intangibles that are so hard to discern but are so terribly important in governing the way people act, the values and norms that are subtly transmitted to individuals and groups and that tend to create binding and bonding.
6. The task of the leader is to lead. And to lead others one must first of all know oneself.[10]

Vision is the decisive element in leading the library. The effective library leader will employ the art of seeing things invisible (seeing around corners), seeing beyond the present, and seeing the possible. A library leader should be able to articulate and formulate strategies that will close the gap between the ideal and the real.

THE SERVICE PHILOSOPHY EXTENDED: THE FUTURE

The future for librarians and libraries has never been brighter. We are entering the most exciting time in our civilization to be a librarian. Technology is a tool that is making our work more effective and giving greater visibility to the service we provide. The fear of technology replacing librarians is baseless; it will enable us to provide more value-added services and free us to become more creative. The value of libraries and librarians to society is much greater than in the past, and will become more so in the future. Many more changes are in store for us. We must learn how to take a leadership role in preparing for and implementing change. Attracting and retaining highly qualified individuals to the profession will remain a challenge.

We can count on the next two decades being a challenging and inspiring time for librarians. Being "a damn good librarian" is a continuous process that we all should hold in our aspirations.

> "I don't know what your destiny will be, but one thing I know: the only ones among you who will be really happy are those who will have sought and found how to serve."
> -- Albert Schweitzer[11]

NOTES

1. Pierce Butler, *An Introduction to Library Science* (Chicago: University of Chicago Press, 1933), xi-xii.

2. Herbert S. White, *Librarians and the Awakening from Innocence: A Collection of Papers by Herbert S. White* (Boston: G. K. Hall, 1989), 143.

3. Rudyard Kipling, "If," *Rudyard Kipling: Complete Verse*, Definitive ed. (New York: Doubleday, 1940), 578, lines 29-32.

4. Fred A. Manske, *Secrets of Effective Leadership* (Memphis: Leadership Education and Development, Inc., 1987), 51.

5. Henry Wadsworth Longfellow, "Morituri Salutamus," *The Complete Poetical Works of Longfellow*, Craigie ed. (Boston: Houghton Mifflin, 1922), 310, stanza 22.

6. Isaac Asimov, "The Permanent Dark Age: Can We Avoid It?" in *Working in the Twenty-First Century*, ed. C. Stewart Sheppard and Donald C. Carroll (New York: John Wiley, 1980), 10.

7. Joanne R. Euster, "Creativity and Leadership," in *Creativity, Innovation, and Entrepreneurship in Libraries*, ed. Donald E. Riggs (New York: Haworth Press, 1989), 36-37.

8. Kathleen Joyce Kruger, "Creativity: An Exploration," in *Creativity, Innovation, and Entrepreneurship in Libraries*, ed. Donald E. Riggs (New York: Haworth Press, 1989), 11.

9. Peter F. Drucker, *Managing for Results: Economic Tasks and Risk-Taking Decisions* (New York: Harper & Row, 1964), 206.

10. Warren G. Bennis, "Where Have All the Leaders Gone?" *Technology Review* 79 (March/April 1977): 45-46.

11. Fred A. Manske, *Secrets of Effective Leadership* (Memphis: Leadership and Development, Inc., 1987), 168.

BIBLIOGRAPHY

Abelson, Philip. "Mechanisms for Evaluating Scientific Information and the Role of Peer Review." *Journal of the American Society for Information Science* 41 (April 1990): 216-222.

"ALA Division Editors: Censored or Edited?" *Library Journal* 115 (March 1, 1990): 54-55.

Alley, Brian, and Jennifer Cargill. "Editing Newsletters and Periodicals." Chap. in *Librarian in Search of Publisher: How to Get Published*, 111-121. Phoenix: Oryx Press, 1986.

American Library Association, Standing Committee on Library Education. "Education for Library and Information Studies in U.S. Universities." Draft distributed May 1991. Cover memo from F. William Summers, Chair.

Armstrong, J. Scott. "Research on Scientific Journals: Implications for Editors and Authors." *Journal of Forecasting* 1 (January - March 1982): 94.

Asimov, Isaac. "The Permanent Dark Age: Can We Avoid It?" In *Working in the Twenty-First Century*, ed. C. Stewart Sheppard and Donald C. Carroll, 1-11. New York: John Wiley, 1980.

Bailar, John C. III, and Kay Patterson. "Journal Peer Review: The Need for a Research Agenda." *New England Journal of Medicine* 312 (March 7, 1985): 654.

Bennis, Warren G. "Where Have All the Leaders Gone?" *Technology Review* 79 (March/April 1977): 37-46.

Berg, A. Scott. *Max Perkins: Editor of Genius*. New York: E. P. Dutton, 1978.

Berry, John N. III. "There's a Candidate on Our Cover." *Library Journal* 115 (March 1, 1990): 4.

Bertalanffy, Ludwig von. *Perspectives on General System Theory: Scientific-Philosophical Studies*. New York: George Braziller, 1975.

Bess, James L. *University Organization: A Matrix Analysis of the Academic Professions*. New York: Human Sciences Press Inc., 1982.

Beyer, Janice M. "Editorial Policies and Practices Among Leading Journals in Four Scientific Fields." *Sociological Quarterly* 19 (Winter 1978): 68-87.

Blake, Virgil L. P., and Renee Tjoumas. "Research as a Factor in Faculty Evaluation: The Rules Are A-Changin'." *Journal of Education for Library and Information Science* 31 (Summer 1990): 3-24.

Boyce, Bert R. "The Institutional Role of the Librarian and Library Educator in the Academic Setting." In *A Service Profession, a Service Commitment: A Festschrift* in Honor of Charles D. Patterson, ed. Connie Van Fleet and Danny P. Wallace, 137-153. Metuchen, NJ: Scarecrow Press, 1992.

Budd, John. "Publication in Library and Information Science: The State of the Literature." *Library Journal* 113 (September 1, 1988): 125-131.

_____. "The Literature of Academic Libraries: An Analysis." *College and Research Libraries* 52 (May 1991): 290-295.

Butler, Pierce. *An Introduction to Library Science*. Chicago: University of Chicago Press, 1933.

Byrne, John A. "Let a Mentor Lead You -- But Beware the Pitfalls," *Business Week* (April 20, 1987): 95.

Cargill, Jennifer. "Developing Library Leaders: The Role of Mentorship." *Library Administration & Management* 3 (Winter 1989): 12-15.

Chatman, Elfreda. "The Role of Mentorship in Shaping Public Library Leaders." *Library Trends* 40 (Winter 1992): 492-512.

Chen, Ching-Chih, and Thomas J. Galvin. "Reviewing the Literature of Librarianship: A State of the Art Report." In *American Reference Books Annual* 1975, ed. Bohdan S. Wynar, xxxi-xlv. Littleton, CO: Libraries Unlimited, 1975.

Cichetti, D. V. "Reliability of Reviews for the *American Psychologist*: A Biostatistical Assessment of the Data." *American Psychologist* 35 (March 1980): 300-303.

Coe, Robert K., and Irwin Weinstock. "Publication Policies of Major Business Journals." *Southern Journal of Business* 3 (January 1968): 1-10.

Craver, Kathleen W. "Book Reviewers: An Empirical Portrait." *School Library Media Quarterly* 12 (Fall 1984): 383-402.

Crawford, Susan, and Loretta Stucki. "Peer Review and the Changing Research Record." *Journal of the American Society for Information Science* 41 (April 1990): 223-228.

Daily, Jay E. "A Happening at College Park, Maryland." *Journal of Education for Librarianship* 9 (Spring 1969): 296-300.

Davis, Donald Gordon Jr. "The Associations of American Library Schools: An Analytical History." PhD. diss., University of Illinois at Urbana-Champaign, 1972.

_____. *The Association of American Library Schools, 1915-1968: An Analytical History*. Metuchen, NJ: Scarecrow Press, 1974.

_____. *Comparative Historical Analysis of Three Association of Professional Schools*. Champaign, IL: University of Illinois Graduate School of Library Science Occasional Papers no. 115, September 1974.

Dickersin, Kay. "The Existence of Publication Bias and Risk Factors for Its Occurrence."*Journal of the American Medical Association* 263 (March 9, 1990): 1385-1389.

Dill, David D. "Research as a Scholarly Activity: Context and Culture." In *Measuring Faculty Research Performance*, ed. John W. Creswell, 7-24. San Francisco: Jossey-Bass Inc., 1986.

Drucker, Peter F. *Managing for Results: Economic Tasks and Risk-taking Decisions*. New York: Harper & Row, 1964.

Ehrenberg, W. "Maxwell's Demon." *Scientific American* 217 (November 1967): 103-110.

Euster, Joanne R. "Creativity and Leadership." In *Creativity, Innovation, and Entrepreneurship in Libraries*, ed. Donald E. Riggs, 27-38. New York: Haworth Press, 1989.

Farren, Caela, Janet Dreyfus Gray, and B. Kaye. "Mentoring: A Boon to Career Development." *Personnel* 61, no. 6 (1984): 20-24.

Ferriero, Davis S. "ARL Directors as Proteges and Mentors." *The Journal of Academic Librarianship* 7 (January 1982): 358-365.

Fiske, Donald W., and Louis Fogg. "But the Reviewers are Making Different Criticisms of My Paper! Diversity and Uniqueness in Reviewer Comments." *American Psychologist* 45 (May 1990): 591-598.

Frantz, Thomas T. "Criteria for Publishable Manuscripts." *Personnel and Guidance Journal* 47 (December 1968): 384-386.

Fritze, Ronald H., Brian E. Coutts, and Louis A. Vyhnanek. *Reference Sources in History: An Introductory Guide*. Santa Barbara, CA: ABC-Clio, 1990.

Futas, Elizabeth. "Faculty Role in Professional Associations: An Answer to Kathleen M. Heim's 'Dimensions of Faculty Public Service: A Policy Science Approach to Questions of Information Provision'." *Journal of Education for library and Information Science* 27 (Winter 1988): 210-215.

Galvin, Thomas J. "AALS and L.E.D.: A Case for Merger." *Journal of Education for Librarianship* 14 (Spring 1974): 211-214.

Gamble, Lynn E. "University Service: New Implications for Academic Librarians." *The Journal for Academic Librarianship* 14 (January 1989): 344-347.

Gehrke, Nathalie. "Toward a Definition of Mentoring." *Theory Into Practice* 27 (Summer 1988): 190-194.

Gerstein, Martin. "Mentoring: An Age Old Practice in a Knowledge-Based Society." Current Trends column in *Journal of Counseling and Development* 64 (October 1985): 156-157.

Glogoff, Stuart. "Reviewing the Gatekeepers: A Survey of Referees of Library Journals." *Journal of the American*

Society for Information Science 39 (November 1988): 400-407.

Gordon, Michael D. "The Role of Referees in Scientific Communication." In *The Psychology of Written Communication*, ed. James Hartley, 263-275. London: Kogen Page, 1980.

Green, Russell G. "Review Bias: Positive or Negative, Good or Bad?" *Behavioral and Brain Sciences* 5 (June 1982): 211.

Hannabuss, Stuart. "Reviewing Reviews." *Signal* 35 (May 1981): 104. Quoted in Grace Hallworth. "Children's Books." In *Reviews and Reviewing: A Guide*, ed. A.J. Walford, 196-213. London: Mansell Publishing, Limited, 1986.

Hardcastle, Beverly. "Spiritual Connections: Proteges' Reflections on Significant Mentorships." *Theory Into Practice* 27 (Summer 1988): 201-208.

Hargens, Lowell L. "Variation in Journal Peer Review Systems." *Journal of the American Medical Association* 263 (March 9, 1990): 1348-1352.

Haring-Hidore, Marilyn. "Mentoring as a Career Enhancement Strategy for Women." *Journal of Counseling and Development* 66 (November 1987): 147-148.

Heim, Kathleen M. "Dimensions of Faculty Public Service: A Policy Science Approach to Questions of Information

Provision." *Journal of Education for Library and Information Science* 26 (Winter 1986): 154-164.

_____. "Refereeing, Scholarly Communication, and the Service Ethos." *RQ* 27 (Summer 1988): 463-466.

_____. "Public Libraries: The Redesign, Reorganization, and Development from a Quarterly to a Bimonthly Publication, June 1988 - December 1989." Report submitted to The Public Library Association. Baton Rouge: Louisiana State University, School of Library and Information Science, Research Center Annex, December 1989.

_____. "Editorial." *Public Libraries* 29 (November/December 1990): 327-328.

Heim, Kathleen, and J. Keith Ostertag, "Sources of Institutional Power: An Analysis of Faculty Policy Participation as an agent of Influence and Domain." *Library Quarterly* 61 (July 1991): 282-290.

Heins, Paul. "Out on a Limb with the Critics: Some Random Thoughts on the Present State of the Criticism of Children's Literature." In *Crosscurrents of Criticism*, ed. Paul Heins, 72-87. Boston: Horn Book, 1977.

Hoge, James O., and James L. W. West III. "Academic Book Reviewing: Some Problems and Suggestions." *Scholarly Publishing* 11 (October 1979): 36.

Houser, L., and Alvin M. Schrader. *The Search for a Scientific Profession: Library Science Education in the*

U.S. and Canada. Metuchen, NJ: Scarecrow Press, 1978.

Hurley, Dan. "The Mentor Mystique." *Psychology Today* 22 (May 1988): 41-43.

Hutchins, Margaret. *Introduction to Reference Work*. Chicago: American Library Association, 1944.

Johnson, Richard D. "The Journal Article." In *Librarian/Author: A Practical Guide on How to Get Published*, ed. Betty-Carol Sellen, 21-35. New York: Neal-Schuman, 1985.

Katz, Bill. "Who is The Reviewer?" *Collection Building* 7 (Spring 1985): 33-35.

Kipling, Rudyard. "If." *Rudyard Kipling: Complete Verse*. Definitive ed. New York: Doubleday, 1940.

Kingsbury, Mary. "How Library Schools Evaluate Faculty Performance." *Journal of Education for Librarianship* 22 (Spring 1982): 219-238.

Kram, Kathy E. "Phases of the Mentor Relationship." *Academy of Management Journal* 26 (December 1983) : 608-625.

Kruger, Kathleen Joyce. "Creativity: An Exploration." In *Creativity, Innovation, and Entrepreneurship in Libraries*, ed. Donald E. Riggs, 3-13. New York: Haworth Press, 1989.

Bibliography

Kuhn, Thomas S. *The Structure of Scientific Revolutions.* 2d ed. Chicago: University of Chicago Press, 1970.

_____. *The Essential Tension: Selected Studies in Scientific Tradition and Change.* Chicago: University of Chicago, 1977.

Lacy, William B., and Lawrence Busch. "Guardians of Science: Journals and Journal Editors in the Agricultural Sciences." *Rural Sociology* 47 (Fall 1982): 429-448.

Lewis, Lionel S. *Scaling the Ivory Tower: Merit and Its Limits in Academic Careers.* Baltimore: John Hopkins University Press, 1975.

Longfellow, Henry Wadsworth. "Morituri Salutamus." *The Complete Poetical Works of Longfellow*, Craigie ed. Boston: Houghton Mifflin, 1992.

Macleod, Beth. "*Library Journal* and *Choice*: A Review of Reviews." *Journal of Academic Librarianship* 7 (March 1981): 23-28.

Mahoney, Michael J. "Publication Prejudices: An Experimental Study of Confirmatory Bias in the Peer Review System." *Cognitive Therapy and Research* 1 (June 1977): 161-175.

Manske, Fred A. *Secrets of Effective Leadership.* Memphis: Leadership Education and Development, Inc., 1987.

McNutt, Robert A., Arthur T. Evans, Robert H. Fletcher, and Suzanne W. Fletcher. "The Effects of Blinding on the

Quality of the Peer Review." *Journal of the American Medical Association* 263 (March 9, 1990): 1371-1376.

Manske, Fred. A. *Secrets of Effective Leadership*. Memphis: Leadership and Development, Inc., 1987.

Mermim, N. David. *Boojums All the Way Through: Communicating Science in a Prosaic Age*. Cambridge: Cambridge University Press, 1990.

Miller, A. Carolyn, and Sharon L. Serzan. "Criteria for Identifying a Refereed Journal." *Journal of Higher Education* 55 (November/December 1984): 677-682.

Mulkay, Michael. *Sociology of Science: A Sociological Pilgrimage*. Buckingham: Open University Press, 1990.

O'Connor, Daniel, and Phyllis Van Orden. "Getting Into Print." *College and Research Libraries* 39 (September 1978): 389-396.

Palmer, Judith L. "A Comparison of Content, Promptness, and Coverage of New Fiction Titles Reviewed in *Library Journal* and *Booklist*, 1964-1984." Vol. 7 *Advances in Library Administration and Organization*. Greenwich, CT: JAI Press, 1988, 89-133.

Paris, Marion. *Library School Closings: Four Case Studies*. Metuchen, NJ: Scarecrow Press, 1988.

Park, Betsy, and Robert Riggs. "Status of the Profession: A 1989 National Survey of Tenure and Promotion Policies for Academic Librarians." *College and Research Libraries* 52 (May 1991): 275-287.

Patterson, Charles D. "An Assessment of the Status of the Journal." *Journal of Education for Library and Information Science* 25 (Spring 1985): 301-311.

_____. "Editorial Accountability: Ethics and Commitment." *Journal of Education for Library and Information Science* 28 (Fall 1987): 83-86.

Pedolsky, Andrea. "Revise and Consent: The Author-Editor Relationship." In *Librarian/Author: A Practical Guide to How to Get Published*, ed. Betty-Carol Sellen, 50-62. New York: Neal-Schuman, 1985.

Peters, Douglas P., and Stephen J. Ceci. "Peer-Review Practices of Psychological Journals: The Fate of Published Articles, Submitted Again." *Behavioral and Brain Science* 5 (June 1982): 187-195.

Plotnik, Art. "Secrets of Writing for the Professional Literature of Librarianship Without Losing Your Self-Esteem." In *Librarian/Author: A Practical Guide on How to Get Published*, ed. Betty-Carol Sellen, 79-90. New York: Neal-Schuman, 1985.

Pool, Gail. "Inside Book Reviewing." In *Library Lit. 18- The Best of 1987*, ed. Bill Katz, 124-132. Metuchen, NJ: Scarecrow Press, 1988.

Prytherch, Ray, ed. *Harrod's Librarians' Glossary*. 6th ed. Brookfield, VT: Gower, 1987.

Riggar, T. F., and R.E. Matkin. "Breaking into Academic Print." *Scholarly Publishing* 22 (October 1990): 17-22.

Sarton, George. "Notes on the Reviewing of Learned Books." *Science* 131 (April 1960): 1182-1187.

Schlachter, Gail. "Reference Books: Editorial." *RQ* 26 (Spring 1987): 382-386.

Schrader, Alvin M. "A Bibliometric Study of JEL, 1960-1984." *Journal of Education for Library and Information Science* 25 (Spring 1985): 279-300.

Seldin, Peter. *Changing Practices in Faculty Evaluation: A Critical Assessment and Recommendations for Improvement.* San Francisco: Jossey-Bass Inc., 1984.

Serebnick, Judith. "Book Reviews and the Selection of Potentially Controversial Books in Public Libraries." *Library Quarterly* 51 (October 1981): 390-409.

Sharp, David W. "What Can and Should Be Done to Reduce Publication Bias? The Perspective of an Editor." *Journal of the American Medical Association* 263 (March 9, 1990): 1390-1391.

Shera, Jesse H. *The Foundations of Education for Librarianship.* New York: John Wiley & Sons, Inc., 1972.

Simon, Rita James, and Linda Mahan. "A Note on the Role of Book Review Editor as Decision Maker." *Library Quarterly* 39 (October 1969): 353-356.

Smith, Alan Jay. "The Task of the Referee." *Computer* 23 (April 1990): 65-71.

Smith, Karen F., Tamara U. Frost, Amy Lyons, and Mary Reichel. "Tenured Librarians in Large University Libraries." *College and Research Libraries* 45 (March 1984): 91-98.

Smith, Lillian H. *The Unreluctant Years: A Critical Approach to Children's Literature*. New York: Viking, 1968.

Spencer, Michael D. G. "Thoroughness of Book Review Indexing: A First Appraisal." *RQ* 26 (Winter 1986): 188-199.

Sperber, Irwin. *Fashions in Science: Opinion Leaders and Collective Behavior in the Social Sciences*. Minneapolis: University of Minnesota Press, 1990.

Stalcup, Sue S. "Mentoring: A Tool for Career Enhancement." *Library Personnel News* 3 (Winter 1989): 4-5.

Stallmann, Esther. "Associations of Professional Schools: A Comparison." *Journal of Education for Librarianship* 1 (Summer 1960): 5-21.

Stephenson, Mary Sue. "Teaching Research Methods in Library and Information Studies Programs." *Journal of Education for Library and Information Science* 31 (Summer 1990): 49-65.

Stone, Elizabeth W. "A Call for the Continued Autonomy and Independence of AALS." *Journal of Education for Librarianship* 14 (Spring 1974): 215-219.

Summers, F. William. "Role of the Association for Library and Information Science Education in Library and Information Science Education." *Library Trends* 34 (Spring 1986): 667-677.

Swoboda, Marion J. and Susan B. Millar. "Networking-Mentoring: Career Strategy of Women in Academic Administration." *Journal of NAWDAC* 49 (1986): 8-13.

Sy, Karen J. "Getting to the Heart of Expert Advice." *Knowledge: Creation, Diffusion, Utilization* 11 (March 1990): 339.

Van Fleet, Connie, and Joan Durrance. "Public Library Leaders and Research: Mechanisms, Perceptions, and Strategies." *Journal of Education for Library and Information Science* 34 (Spring 1993): in press.

Webreck, Susan J., and Judith Weedman. "Professional Library Literature: An Analysis of the Review Literature." Vol. 2, *Library Science Annual*. Littleton, CO: Libraries Unlimited, 1986, 3-12.

White, Herbert S. *Librarians and the Awakening from Innocence: A Collection of Papers by Herbert S. White*. Boston: G.K. Hall, 1989.

Wight, Edward A. "Standards and Stature in Librarianship." *Journal of Education for Librarianship* 2 (Fall 1961): 59-67.

Wilson, Louis R. "Historical Development of Education for Librarianship in the United States." In *Education for Librarianship; Papers Presented at the Library Conference, University of Chicago, August 16-21, 1948*, ed. Bernard Berelson, 44-65. Chicago: American Library Association, 1949.

Wilson, Pauline. "Factors Effecting Research Productivity." *Journal of Education for Librarianship* 20 (Summer 1979): 3-24.

Winger, Howard W. "AALS Publishing in the 50s: Predecessors of JEL." *Journal of Education for Library and Information Science* 25 (Spring 1985): 245-261.

Wolper, Roy S. "On Academic Reviewing: Ten Common Errors." *Scholarly Publishing* 16 (April 1985): 269-275.

Wong, Paul T. P. "Implicit Editorial Policies and the Integrity of Psychology as an Empirical Science." *American Psychologist* 36 (June 1981): 690-691.

Woodring, Paul. "Some Thoughts on Book Reviewing." *Phi Delta Kappan* 63 (February 1982): 422.

Yamamoto, Kaoru. "To See Life Grow: The Meaning of Mentorship." *Theory Into Practice* 27 (Summer 1988): 183-189.

Zey, Michael. *The Mentor Connection*. Homewood, Ill: Dow-Jones-Irwin, 1984.

Ziman, John M. *Public Knowledge: An Essay Concerning the Social Dimension of Science*. Cambridge: Cambridge University Press, 1968.

PUBLICATIONS OF CHARLES D. PATTERSON

BOOKS, CHAPTERS, AND ARTICLES

Patterson, Charles D. "Origins of Systematic Serials Control: Remembering Carolyn Ulrich." In *Reference and Information Services: A Reader for the Nineties*, 351-379. Metuchen, NJ & London: Scarecrow Press, 1991.

_____. "Resource Materials." In *The Video Annual, 1991*, 145-177. Santa Barbara, CA: ABC-CLIO Press, 1991.

_____. "Library User Instruction in the Curriculum: Background and Status Update." In *Continuing Education of Reference Librarians*, 83-96. New York: The Haworth Press, 1990.

_____. "Carolyn Farquhar Ulrich (1880-1969)." In *Dictionary of American Library Biography*, 136-138, 1st supp. Littleton, CO: Libraries Unlimited, 1990.

_____. "Library User Instruction in the Curriculum: Background and Status Update." *The Reference Librarian* 30 (1990): 83-96.

_____, and Donna W. Howell. "Library User Education: Assessing the Attitudes of Those Who Teach." *RQ* 29 (Summer 1990): 513-524.

_____. "Origins of Systematic Serials Control: Remembering Carolyn Ulrich." *Reference Services Review* 16, no. 1-2 (Spring/Summer 1988): 79-92. This article was sent world wide to subscribers of *Ulrich's International Periodicals Directory* by publishers R.R. Bowker Company.

_____, and Donald Davis, Jr. *ARBA Guide to Library Science Literature 1970-1983*. Littleton, CO: Libraries Unlimited, 1987.

_____. "Editorial Accountability: Ethics and Commitment." *Journal of Education for Library and Information Science* 28 (Fall 1987): 83-86.

_____. "Librarians as Teachers: A Component of the Educational Process." *Journal of Education for Library and Information Science* 28 (Summer 1987): 3-8.

_____. "The Name Behind the Title: Joseph Whitaker--Still An Annual Affair." *Reference Services Review* 15 (Spring 1987): 67-69.

_____. "The Crisis in Our Schools and in Professional Education." *Journal of Education for Library and Information Science* 27 (Fall 1986): 67-70.

_____. "The Problems Persist and the Challenge Continues." *Journal of Education for Library and Information Science* 26 (Spring 1986): 211-214.

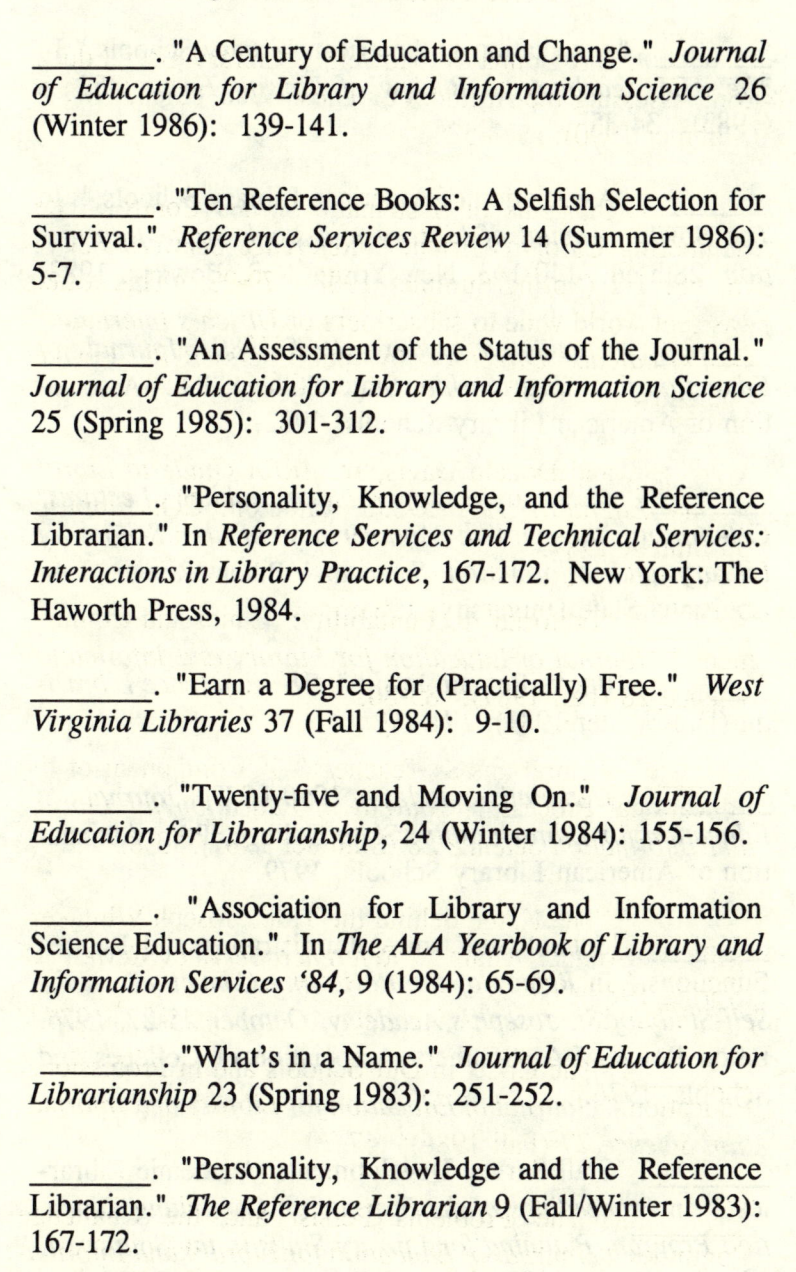

_____. "A Century of Education and Change." *Journal of Education for Library and Information Science* 26 (Winter 1986): 139-141.

_____. "Ten Reference Books: A Selfish Selection for Survival." *Reference Services Review* 14 (Summer 1986): 5-7.

_____. "An Assessment of the Status of the Journal." *Journal of Education for Library and Information Science* 25 (Spring 1985): 301-312.

_____. "Personality, Knowledge, and the Reference Librarian." In *Reference Services and Technical Services: Interactions in Library Practice*, 167-172. New York: The Haworth Press, 1984.

_____. "Earn a Degree for (Practically) Free." *West Virginia Libraries* 37 (Fall 1984): 9-10.

_____. "Twenty-five and Moving On." *Journal of Education for Librarianship*, 24 (Winter 1984): 155-156.

_____. "Association for Library and Information Science Education." In *The ALA Yearbook of Library and Information Services '84*, 9 (1984): 65-69.

_____. "What's in a Name." *Journal of Education for Librarianship* 23 (Spring 1983): 251-252.

_____. "Personality, Knowledge and the Reference Librarian." *The Reference Librarian* 9 (Fall/Winter 1983): 167-172.

_____. "Association of American Library Schools." In *The ALA Yearbook, a Review of Library Events '83*, 8 (1983): 34-35.

_____. "Association of American Library Schools," In *The Bowker Annual of Library and Book Trade Information*, 28th ed., 140-143, New York: R.R. Bowker, 1983.

_____. *Cumulative Index, 1975-1980, Journal of Education for Librarianship*. State College, PA: Association of American Library Schools, 1982.

_____, ed. and comp. *Golden Jubilee Lectures: Celebrating the Fiftieth Anniversary of the School of Library and Information Science*. Baton Rouge, LA: Louisiana State University, 1981.

_____. "Books Remain Basic." *The Reference Librarian* (Fall/Winter 1981): 171-172.

_____. *Cumulative Index, 1960-1975, Journal of Education for Librarianship*. State College, PA: Association of American Library Schools, 1979.

_____. "School Staff and Administration and Related Functions." In *Report of the Reviewing Committee on the Self-Study of St. Joseph's Academy, October 25-27, 1976*. Baton Rouge, LA: Southern Association of Colleges and Schools, 1976.

_____. "Staff Survey Development: Academic Libraries." In *Proceedings of the Institute on Continuing Education Program Planning for Library Staffs in the Southwest, March 17-28, 1975*. Baton Rouge: LSU/GSLS and

SWLA, June, 1975. Also appears in the revised edition August, 1975.

_____. "Margaret Hutchins." In *Encyclopedia of Library and Information Sciences, Vol. 11*, 123-127. New York: Marcel Dekker, Inc., 1974.

_____. *Library of Congress Music Subject Headings*. Pittsburgh: University of Pittsburgh Dissertation Series, 1971.

_____. "The Seminar Method in Library Education." *Journal of Education for Librarianship* 8 (Fall 1967): 99-105.

_____. "The Book Collecting of Arthur Dayton." *West Virginia Libraries* 19 (September 1966): 11-23.

_____. "The Library Idea." *West Virginia Libraries* 18 (December 1965): 1-2.

_____. "A West Virginia Library in Sweden." *West Virginia Libraries* 18 (September 1965): 2-4.

_____. "West Virginia Needs Librarians -- An Editorial." *West Virginia School Journal* 18 (April 1964): 2-4.

_____. "Recruitment Network in West Virginia." *West Virginia Libraries* 16 (December 1963): 15-19.

_____. "Research in Librarianship at West Virginia University." *West Virginia Libraries* 16 (September 1963): 11-13.

_____. "A Library for the School." *West Virginia School Journal* 91 (November 1962): 8 ff., 24.

_____. "Observations on Recruiting." *West Virginia Libraries* 14 (June 1961): 11-16.

_____. "All Paths Lead to the Library." *West Virginia School Journal* 89 (January 1961):16, 31.

BOOK REVIEWS (A Partial Listing)

Patterson, Charles D. Review of "An Uncertain Crusade: The History of Library Use Instruction in a Changing Educational Environment," by Larry Hardesty and John Tucker. In *Academic Librarianship: Past, Present, and Future. A Festschrift in Honor of David Kaser.* In *Research Strategies* (Fall 1991): 206-208.

_____. Review of *Education of Library and Information Professionals: Present and Future Prospects*, ed. Richard K. Gardner. In *Journal of the American Society for Information Science* (March 1990): 148.

_____. Review of *Publishing and Review of Reference Sources*, ed. Bill Katz and Robin Kinder. In *Information Processing and Management* 24, no.2 (1988): 209-210.

_____. Review of *Education of Library and Information Professionals: Present and Future Prospects*, ed. Richard K. Gardner. In *Library Journal* (January 1988): 62.

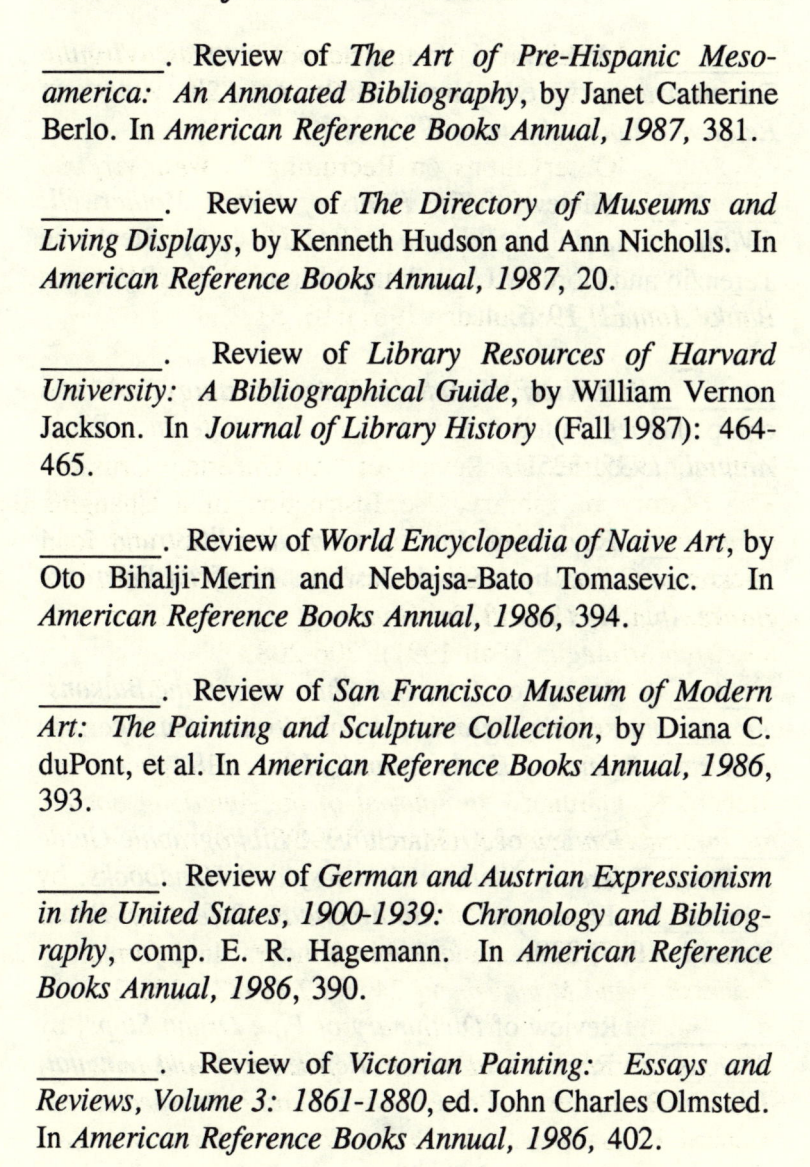

_____. Review of *The Art of Pre-Hispanic Mesoamerica: An Annotated Bibliography*, by Janet Catherine Berlo. In *American Reference Books Annual, 1987*, 381.

_____. Review of *The Directory of Museums and Living Displays*, by Kenneth Hudson and Ann Nicholls. In *American Reference Books Annual, 1987*, 20.

_____. Review of *Library Resources of Harvard University: A Bibliographical Guide*, by William Vernon Jackson. In *Journal of Library History* (Fall 1987): 464-465.

_____. Review of *World Encyclopedia of Naive Art*, by Oto Bihalji-Merin and Nebajsa-Bato Tomasevic. In *American Reference Books Annual, 1986*, 394.

_____. Review of *San Francisco Museum of Modern Art: The Painting and Sculpture Collection*, by Diana C. duPont, et al. In *American Reference Books Annual, 1986*, 393.

_____. Review of *German and Austrian Expressionism in the United States, 1900-1939: Chronology and Bibliography*, comp. E. R. Hagemann. In *American Reference Books Annual, 1986*, 390.

_____. Review of *Victorian Painting: Essays and Reviews, Volume 3: 1861-1880*, ed. John Charles Olmsted. In *American Reference Books Annual, 1986*, 402.

_____. Review of *The Oxford Companion to the Decorative Arts*, ed. Harold Osborne. In *American Reference Books Annual, 1986*, 365.

_____. Review of *The Prints of Robert Motherwell: [With] A Catalogue Raisonne 1943-1984*, by Stephanie Terenzio and Dorothy C. Belknap. In *American Reference Books Annual, 1986*, 401.

_____. Review of *American Art Directory*, ed. and comp. Jaques Cattell Press. In *American Reference Books Annual, 1985*, 325.

_____. Review of *American Popular Illustration: A Reference Guide*, by James J. Best. In *American Reference Books Annual, 1985*, 328.

_____. Review of *Art and Architecture in the Balkans: An Annotated Bibliography*, by Slobodan Curcic. In *American Reference Books Annual, 1985*, 319.

_____. Review of *Architecture: A Bibliographic Guide to Basic Reference Works, Histories, and Handbooks*, by Donald L. Ehresmann. In *American Reference Books Annual, 1985*, 330.

_____. Review of *Dictionary of Pipe Organ Stops*, by Stevens Irwin. In *American Reference Books Annual, 1985*, 427.

_____. Review of *Evaluation of Reference Services*, ed. Bill Katz and Ruth A. Fraley. In *Journal of the

American Society for Information Science 36 (November 1985), 418-419.

_____. Review of *Four Centuries of Organ Music: From the Roberts-Bridge Codex Through the Baroque Era*, by Marilou Kratzenstein and Jerald Hamilton. In *American Reference Books Annual, 1985*, 427.

_____. Review of *The New Grove Second Viennese School: Schoenberg, Webern, Berg*, by Oliver Neighbour, Paul Griffiths and George Perle. In *American Reference Books Annual, 1985*, 432.

_____. Review of *Book Illustrators of the Twentieth Century*, by Brigid Peppin and Lucy Micklethwait. In *American Reference Books Annual, 1985*, 337.

_____. Review of *The Realist Debate: A Bibliography of French Realist Painting, 1830-1885*, by Yvonne M. L. Weisberg and Gabriel P. Weisberg. In *American Reference Books Annual, 1985*, 339.

_____. Review of *Who's Who in Art*. In *American Reference Books Annual, 1985*, 321.

_____. Review of *Frida Kahlo: A Bibliography*, by Rupert Garcia. In *American Reference Books Annual, 1984*, 403.

_____. Review of *Hieronymus Bosch: An Annotated Bibliography*, by Walter S. Gibson. In *American Reference Books Annual, 1984*, 404.

_____. Review of *The Texas Art Review*, by Les Krantz. In *American Reference Books Annual, 1984*, 393.

_____. Review of *The Georgia Catalog, Historic American Buildings Survey: A Guide to the Architecture of the State*, by John Linley. In *American Reference Books Annual, 1984*, 399.

_____. Review of *World Art in American Museums: A Personal Guide*, by Richard McLanathan. In *American Reference Books Annual, 1984*, 394.

_____. Review of *Dugento Painting: An Annotated Bibliography*, by James H. Stubblebine. In *American Reference Books Annual, 1984*, 405.

_____. Review of *Dictionary of Contemporary American Artists*, by Paul Cummings. In *American Reference Books Annual, 1983*, 400.

_____. Review of *Dante Gabriel Rossetti: An Annotated Bibliography*, by Francis L. Fennell. In *American Reference Books Annual, 1983*, 398.

_____. Review of *Museums Discovered: The Brucke Museum*, by Leopold Reidemeister. In *American Reference Books Annual, 1983*, 387.

_____. Review of *The Lyle Official Antiques Review*, comp. Margot Rutherford, ed. Anthony Curtis. In *American Reference Books Annual, 1983*, 404-405.

_____. Review of *Ludwig Karl Hilberseimer: An Annotated Bibliography and Chronology*, by David Spaeth. In *American Reference Books Annual, 1983*, 394.

_____. Review of *Tours and Visits Directory: A Behind-The-Scenes Guide to Factories, Mines, Business Firms, Government Agencies, Cultural and Educational Institutions, and Other Facilities which Receive Visitors*, ed. Gale Research Inc. In *American Reference Books Annual*, 1983, 264-265.

_____. Review of *World Museum Publications: A Directory of Art and Cultural Museums, Their Publications and Audio-Visual Materials, 1982*, ed. R. R. Bowker. In *American Reference Books Annual,, 1983*, 390.

_____. Review of *Curator's Choice: An Introduction to the Art Museums of the U. S.: Four Volumes*, by Babbette Brant Fromme. In *American Reference Books Annual, 1982*, 461.

_____. Review of *The Penguin Dictionary of Architecture*, by John Fleming, Hugh Honor and Nikolaus Pevsner. *American Reference Books Annual, 1982*, 468.

_____. Review of *Lyle Antiques Identification Guide*, Lyle Publication. In *American Reference Books Annual, 1982*, 482.

_____. Review of *Identifying American Furniture: A Pictorial Guide to Styles and Terms, Colonial to Contemporary*, by Milo M. Naeve. In *American Reference Books Annual, 1982*, 487.

_____. Review of *Contemporary British Artists*, ed. Charlotte Parry-Cooke. In *American Reference Books Annual, 1981*, 427.

_____. Review of *Musical Instruments of the World: An Illustrated Encyclopedia*, by the Diagram Group. In *American Reference Books Annual, 1980*, 437.

_____. Review of *Dictionary of Terms in Music: English-German / German-English*, ed. Horst Leuchtmann. In *American Reference Books Annual, 1979*, 470.

_____. Review of *Museums in New York*, by Fred W. McDarrah. In *American Reference Books Annual, 1979*, 46.

_____. Review of *The American Humanities Index for 1975, Volume I*, ed. Whitston Pub. Co. Inc. In *American Reference Books Annual, 1978*, 13.

_____. Review of *Louisiana Almanac, 1973-1974*, ed. James Calhoun and assoc. ed. Helen Kerr Kempe. In *American Reference Books Annual, 1976*, 259.

_____. Review of *The Typographical Gazetteer*, by Henry Cotton. In *American Reference Books Annual, 1977*, 424.

_____. Review of *A Survey of Musical Instruments*, by Sibyl Marcuse. In *Booklist* (March 1, 1977): 1037.

_____. Review of *Music Titles in Translation*, comp. Julian Hogson. In *Booklist* (February 15, 1977): 926.

_____. Review of *Translator Referral Directory, 1975-1976*, comp. Guild of Professional Translators. In *American Reference Books Annual, 1977*, 516.

_____. Review of *A Descriptive Index to Shakespeare's Characters in Shakespear's Words*, by Walter Jerrold. In *American Reference Books Annual, 1977*, 603.

_____. Review of *The Music Guide to Great Britain: England, Scotland, Wales, Ireland*, ed. Elaine Brody and Claire Brook. In *Booklist* (May 15, 1976): 1369.

_____. Review of *National Radio Publicity Directory, 74-75: Cross-Referenced Information on Network, Syndicated and Local Talk Shows From All 50 States Including College Stations*, ed. Cheryl Filsinger, Marle Becker and David Richmond associates. In *American Reference Books Annual, 1976*, 566.

_____. Review of *International Who's Who in Music and Musicians' Directory*, ed. Ernest Kay. In *Booklist* (May 15, 1976): 1368.

_____. Review of *Art and Indian Individualists: The Art of Seventeen Contemporary Southwestern Artists and Craftsmen*, by Guy Monthan and Doris Monthan. In *American Reference Books Annual*, 1976, 444.

_____. Review of *Museums USA: Purposes and Functions, Programs, Attendance, Accessibility, Admissions, Collections and Exhibitions, Trustees, Personnel, Facilities, Finances*, by National Endowment for the Arts. In *American Reference Books Annual, 1976*, 64.

_____. Review of *Petrarch: Catalogues of the Petrarch Collection in Cornell University Library*. In *American Reference Books Annual, 1976*, 626.

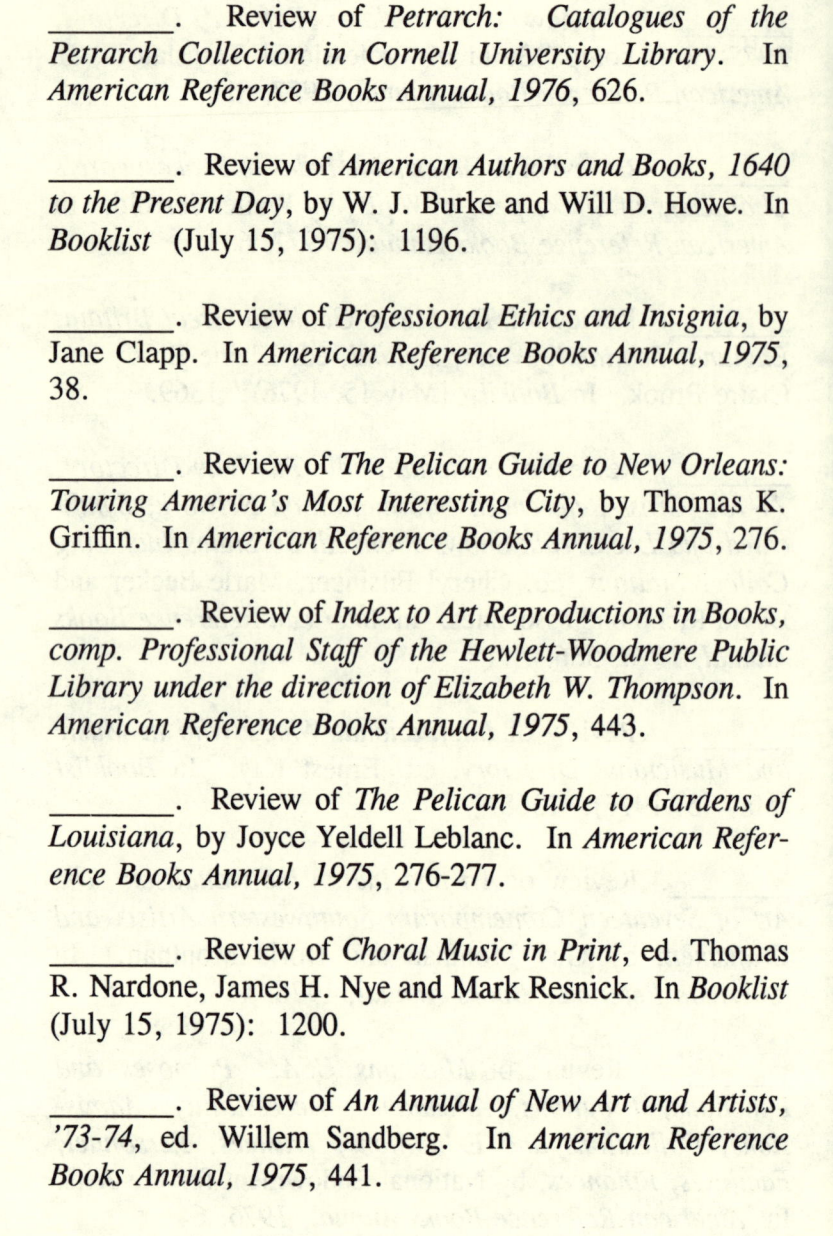

_____. Review of *American Authors and Books, 1640 to the Present Day*, by W. J. Burke and Will D. Howe. In *Booklist* (July 15, 1975): 1196.

_____. Review of *Professional Ethics and Insignia*, by Jane Clapp. In *American Reference Books Annual, 1975*, 38.

_____. Review of *The Pelican Guide to New Orleans: Touring America's Most Interesting City*, by Thomas K. Griffin. In *American Reference Books Annual, 1975*, 276.

_____. Review of *Index to Art Reproductions in Books*, comp. Professional Staff of the Hewlett-Woodmere Public Library under the direction of Elizabeth W. Thompson. In *American Reference Books Annual, 1975*, 443.

_____. Review of *The Pelican Guide to Gardens of Louisiana*, by Joyce Yeldell Leblanc. In *American Reference Books Annual, 1975*, 276-277.

_____. Review of *Choral Music in Print*, ed. Thomas R. Nardone, James H. Nye and Mark Resnick. In *Booklist* (July 15, 1975): 1200.

_____. Review of *An Annual of New Art and Artists, '73-74*, ed. Willem Sandberg. In *American Reference Books Annual, 1975*, 441.

_____. Review of *Whole Grains: A Book of Quotations*, ed. Art Spiegleman and Bob Schneider. In *American Reference Books Annual, 1975*, 43.

_____. Review of *Periodicals in Humanities: Union Catalogue of Periodicals in Humanities and Newspapers in Delhi Libraries*, by J. A. Wajid and H. K. Kaul. In *American Reference Books Annual, 1975*, 20.

_____. Review of *Reader in Music Librarianship*, ed. C. J. Bradley. In *Library Journal* (July 1974): 1783.

_____. Review of *What They Said in 1972: The Yearbook of Spoken Opinion*, ed. and comp. Alan F. Pater and Jason R. Pater. In *American Reference Books Annual, 1974*, 31.

_____. Review of *Allen's Synonyms and Antonyms*, by F. Sturges Allen. In *American Reference Books Annual, 1973*, 455

_____. Review of *Reference Services for Undergraduate Students: Four Case Studies*, by Billy R. Wilkinson. In *American Reference Books Annual, 1973*, 79.

INDEX

Abelson, Philip 58
Academic Common Market v
Academic librarians xii, 43, 44, 137-139, 141, 142, 150, 151
    surveys 44
Academic libraries 9, 142, 144
    directors 77
Advertising 8
Advising 139, 142, 146, 147, 155-159, 161, 163, 169, 171, 173
    benefits 158
    definition 156-157
    programs 171
    See also Faculty responsibilities; Mentoring
ALA Yearbook vi
Alley, Brian 13
American Association of University Professors viii
American Library Association viii, xii, 6, 71, 75, 76, 77, 81, 98, 122, 124, 130, 131, 132
    accreditation of library and information science programs 24, 77, 78, 82, 89, 104, 106, 107, 109, 124, 125
    American Library History Round Table 134
    Award for Distinguished Service to Education for Librarianship 125

Index

    Beta Phi Mu Award vii, 127-128
    Board of Education for Librarianship 77
    conferences 107, 108, 120, 121
    Intellectual Freedom Committee 134
    Library Education Division 72, 76, 81
    Louis Shores-Oryx Press Award 87
    publications 8, 44
    Publishing Services Division 133
    Standing Committee on Library Education (SCOLE) 6

American Reference Books Annual vii
American Society for Information Science 97
Andragogy 97, 156
Appell, Alice 105, 108
Armstrong, J. Scott 61
Asimov, Isaac 190
Association for Library and Information Science Education viii, ix, xii, 71-99
    committee chairs 90-96, 99
    committee members 84, 91-96, 98
    committees 72, 77, 96
    history 71, 79, 82, 93, 98
    officers 80, 84, 87, 89, 91, 92, 94-99
    special interest group conveners 84, 92-93, 95-96, 98
Association of American Library Schools
    See Association for Library and Information Science Education
Association of College and Research Libraries
    Tri-State Chapter vi
Association of College Honor Societies 123
Atcheson, Jean 105
Audience 3, 7, 8, 11, 14, 26, 29, 32, 36-37
    definition 4, 8, 9, 13

professional/technical 4
universal 4

Bailar, John C. III 52
Bailey, George M. 119
Bemidji State University iv, v
Bennis, Warren G. 194
Bentz, Dale M. 119
Bess, James L. 142
Beta Phi Mu iii, vii, viii, xii, 104-136
    Ad Hoc Committee on Speakers Bureau 123
    ad hoc committees 122-123
    administrative secretary 117
    advisory assembly 115-117, 120-121, 135
    Alpha Chapter 108
    associate executive secretary 108
    Award for Distinguished Service to Education for Librarianship 124
    Beta Chapter 108
    Beta Zeta Chapter vii, 135
    board of governors **See** executive council
    budget 116, 117
    by-laws 105, 109, 115, 116, 121
    Certificate of Distinction 129
    chapbook series 129-132
    chapter charters 108, 109, 115
    chapters 107, 108-115, 116, 117, 118, 120, 121, 123, 129, 135
    committees 108, 117, 121-123, 129
    constitution 105, 108
    Delta Chapter 108
    directors 116-118, 121, 135

Index

Distinguished Lecture Series 122
Documents Committee 121
dues 115
Epsilon Chapter 108
executive council 107-109, 115-117, 120-122, 124, 127, 132-135
executive director 107
executive secretary 116-117, 121, 125, 126
faculty advisers 115
Frank B. Sessa Scholarship 125
Gamma Chapter 108
Harold Lancour Scholarship for Foreign Study 126
honorary membership 107
past president 116, 122
initiation 105-108, 115-117, 120, 129, 124
insignia 106
international chapters 106-108
international membership 107
invitation criteria 106-107
joint chapters 109
meetings 108, 116-117, 120-121, 134
mission 106
monograph series 122, 132-133
Monograph Series Editorial Board 122
national headquarters 116-117, 121, 133
National Membership Committee 108
newsletters 106, 117, 122, 129
Nominating Committee 122
officers 105, 107, 115, 117, 118, 129
origin of name 105
president 105, 108, 116-122, 124-126
professional chapters 109
Public Affairs Committee 122

publications 106, 116, 129-133
Publications Committee 130
purposes 104-106
records and archives 117
Sarah Rebecca Reed Scholarship 124-125
scholarships and awards 106, 116, 120, 122, 124-128, 135
scholarships and awards -- recipients 125-129
Scholarships and Grants Committee 122
special awards 128
Task Force on the Future of Beta Phi Mu 123
tax exempt status 123
treasurer 105, 108, 116-117
vice-president/president-elect 105, 108, 116-117

Beta Phi Mu Award 127, 135
Beta Phi Mu Award for Excellence in Professional Writing 128
Beta Phi Mu Good Teaching Award 128
Beta Phi Mu Newsletter 122, 129
Beta Zetings vii
Beyer, Janice M. 45, 47-49
Bhagavad Gita 3
Bible 3
Bibliometrics 73, 86, 9 **See also** Citation analysis
Bildung des Bibliothekars 106
Boaz, Martha 118
Bomar, Cora Paul 119
Booklist vii, 29, 30
Bowker Annual vi
Boyce, Bert R. 93, 94
Boyd, Anne M. 105

Index

Brown, Dee A. 118, 129
Brown, George B. 105
Browning, Robert 131
Budd, John M. 9-11
Busch, Lawrence 46
Business education 192-193
Butler, Pierce 179

Campbell, Bruce 131
Canadian Library Association 134
Career development 3, 170
Cargill, Jennifer 13
Carroll, Frances Laverne 131
CD-ROM database reviews 20
    See also Databases; Software Reviews
Ceci, Stephen J. 57
Chatman, Elfreda 120
Chen, Ching-chih 27
Cheney, Frances Neel 118, 120
Choice 30-32
Cichetti, D. V. 54
Citation analysis 4, 9 **See also** Bibliometrics
Citation indexes 4
Coe, Robert K. 53
Cole, John Y. 134
Collection development 20, 21, 23, 24, 28, 31, 32, 37
Columbia University 104
Column editors 14 **See also** Editors
Columns 14, 35, 84, 87-88, 95-96
Consultants and consulting 18, 36, 137-139, 144, 147, 150 **See also** Professional service
Continuing education 124, 125, 128, 186, 188
    See also Library and information science education

Cooper, Alice 105
Coutts, Brian E. 168
Creativity 46, 80, 129, 184, 189-192, 195
Criticism 3, 12, 21-22, 33
    See also Reviews and reviewing

Daily, Jay 82, 97
Databases 4, 20 **See also** CD-ROM database reviews;
    Software reviews
Davis, Donald G. 72, 75, 93, 98, 99
DeLaMare-Schaefer, Mary 169
Delzell, Robert F. 119
Dickersin, Kay 55
Dictionary of American Biography vi
Doms, Keith 119
Downs, Robert B. 105

Ebert, Friedrich Adolph 106
Eckerstrom, Ralph 129
Editing xi, 2-15, 138
    ethics 2, 15, 54
    process 12, 45-46
Editorial boards 5, 8-11, 13, 15, 54, 122
Editorial policies 5, 11, 13, 23, 24, 32, 33, 36, 47, 49,
    52, 61-65, 87
Editors 2-18, 20, 28, 33-36, 44, 43-49, 50, 51, 53, 54,
    60, 63
    library and information science 2, 4, 6-10, 12, 13,
        15, 64
    See also Column editors; Editing; Review editors
Emporia State University 124
Entropy 60-62
Euster, Joanne R. 190

Index 237

Faculty development 150
Faculty evaluation 24-27, 74, 141-142, 145-146, 148-150
    surveys 27
Faculty governance 138, 139, 141-146, 148
Faculty responsibilities 24, 48, 93-95, 97, 137-151, 156-159, 171
    See also Advising
Fiske, Donald W. 54
Florida State University 108
Fogg, Louis 55
Ford, Stephen 119
Frantz, Thomas J. 54
Fraud 58, 59
Fritze, Ronald H. 168
Funding for research 58, 9, 106, 126, 144
    See also Grant proposals

Galvin, Thomas J. 26, 75
Gamble, Lynn E. 142
Gatekeeper function 42, 44-47
Gehrke, Nathalie 166
Gift-exchange model **See** Mentoring
Glenville State College v
Glogoff, Stuart 52
Gordon, Michael D. 53
Governor's Conference on Library and Information Services viii
Grant proposals 137 **See also** Funding for research
Grant, Isabelle 118
Green, Russell G. 57
Grooming-mentoring **See** Mentoring

H. M. "Hub" Cotton Faculty Excellence Award viii

Hannabuss, Stuart 22
Hargens, Lowell L. 63
Harrar, H. Joanne 121
Harrison, J. Clement 108
Heim, Kathleen M. 139, 143, 144
Holley, Edward G. 121, 134
Horrocks, Norman 120
Houser, Lloyd 72
Hunt, Mary Alice 118
Hurley, Dan 172
Hutchins, Margaret 32
Iben, Icko 105

*I*mage 189
Informal communication 42, 163
    See also Scholarly communication
Information Processing and Management vii
Information theory 60
Instructions to authors 4 **See also** Editing, Editors
Intellectual freedom 123, 134

*J*ackson, William V. 119
Jesse, William 105
Johnson, Richard D. 13
Journal of Education for Librarianship
    See *Journal of Education for Library and Information Science*
Journal of Education for Library and Information Science
    vi, ix, xi, 8, 15, 71, 73, 75, 78, 84, 86, 87, 91, 93, 126, 134
    authors 73, 84-86, 95-96
    bibliometric analysis 73, 86, 93
    column contributors 84, 87-89, 95-96

Index

Journal of Library History vii, 135
Journal of the American Society for Information Science vii
Journals
    growth 42, 44
    impact and importance 4, 42, 43, 46
    quality control 45, 51, 62
    roles and functions 46, 47, 62, 64
    See also Library and information science literature

Kaser, David 119, 132
Katz, Bill 37
Keele, Reba 169
Keller, Helen i
Kingsbury, Mary 24, 141
Kipling, Rudyard 184
Knapp, Patricia B. 128
Kruger, Kathleen Joyce 191
Kuhn, Thomas S. 47-48

Lacy, William B. 45
Lancour, Harold 104, 105, 107, 108, 117, 126, 128, 129
"Landmarks of Reference" vi
Leadership i, xii, 71, 73, 78-83, 94, 96-99, 116, 123, 124, 132, 148, 155, 160, 173, 185, 188, 189, 192, 193-195
Lewis, Lionel S. 140
Library and information science education ii, xii, 6, 8, 24, 43, 44, 71-99, 105-107, 137, 139, 141, 142, 145-146, 148, 150, 178, 180, 186-188, 191, 193-194
    administration 82, 83, 89, 94-98, 142, 145-246, 178, 180, 186-188, 193-194

See also Association for Library and Information Science Education; Continuing education; *Journal of Education for Library and Information Science Research*

Library and information science literature 8, 26, 27, 30, 32, 43, 44, 49, 52-54, 59, 60, 73, 86, 162
   growth 44
   See also Titles of specific publications

Library and Information Science Research 6, 7, 12, 73, 133

Library and information science theory 179
Library History Seminar V 134
Library History Seminar VI 134
Library Journal 8, 29-32
Library Quarterly, The 8, 10
Library Trends 127
Lodge, Louise 105
Lohrer, Alice 119
Longfellow, Henry Wadsworth 186
Loughborough College of Librarianship 108
Louisiana Library Association viii
Louisiana State University v, vi, vii, viii, 135
Luther, Kathryn 105

Macleod, Beth 30-32
Madonna i
Mahoney, Michael J. 57
Manchester School of Librarianship 108
Manuscripts
      acceptance rates 9, 11, 54
      preparation 3, 14, 15
      review process 50-53, 55, 57, 63, 64
      revision 3, 5, 12, 13

       selection 9-12, 55, 60, 64
       solicitation 4, 5, 15
       submission rates 9
       See also Editing; Referees and refereeing; Reviews and reviewing
Manutius, Aldus 106
Market economy model **See** Mentoring
Mauss, Marcel 162
Maxwell, James Clerk 60
Maxwell's Demon 59-61, 64
McNutt, Robert A. 51
Mentoring viii, 155-173, 181
       benefits 161, 167, 169
       conditions 166, 167
       definition 161
       gift exchange model 162, 166-170
       grooming-mentoring 162, 168-170
       market economy model 162-165, 167, 169-170
       networking-mentoring model 170
       phases 164, 165
       risks 165
       See also Advising; Faculty Responsibilities
Mermin, David 42, 43
Miami Public Library 126
Mika, Joseph J. 120
Millar, Susan B. 170

*N*etworking-mentoring model **See** Mentoring

*O*ller, A. Kathryn 119
Ostertag, J. Keith 143, 144

Pali Canon 3
Palmer, Judith L. 29
Paradigms 47-49, 52
Paris, Marion 142
Park, Betsy 44
Patterson, Charles D. ii, iv, v, vi, vii, viii, ix, xi, xii, 8, 9, 15, 135, 154, 168
Patterson, Charles Irwin iv
Patterson, Inez Fern (Slagg) iv
Patterson, Kay 52
Pedolsky, Andrea 3
Peer review **See** Referees and refereeing
Pennsylvania Library Association vi
Perkins, Max 2, 3
Personnel training 160
Peters, Douglas P. 57
Phelps, Rose B. 105
Plotnik, Art 6
Pool, Gail 33
Professional associations i, xii, 8, 19, 73, 78, 79, 97, 137-139, 141, 144, 147, 148, 150, 188-189, 191
    publications i, xi, 47
    See also Names of specific associations
Professional commitment xii, 27, 28, 30, 48, 63, 64, 106, 183, 185, 188
Professional ethics i, 15
Professional service xii, 15, 24, 36, 37, 60, 64, 54, 94, 96-99, 137, 128, 137-151, 178-185
    evaluation 146, 148-150
    off-campus 138-141, 147
    on-campus 138, 139, 141-148, 188-189
Promotion and tenure 6, 139, 141, 146, 148
Public Libraries 8, 10, 14

Index

Publication delays 6, 11
Pumphrey, Virginia 105

*Q*ua'an 3

*R*amsey, Jack 118
Reader surveys 8, 9
Reed, Sarah Rebecca 119, 124
Referees and refereeing ii, xi, 5, 9-12, 14, 42-65, 87, 137, 143 87, 137, 143
    benefits 10, 49, 52
    library and information science 44, 52, 54, 60
    negative aspects 54
    surveys 51-57, 61
    See also Editing
Reference Librarian, The vi
Reference Services Review vi
Research Strategies vii
Review editors 20, 34, 35 **See also** Editors
Reviewers ii, 20, 22
    authority 30
    professional 19, 28, 29, 36
    qualifications 22, 24, 32
    surveys 23, 33
    volunteer 19, 20, 25, 27-29, 35, 36
Reviews and reviewing xi, 14, 15, 19-38
    classroom applications 21
    collection development 20, 21, 23, 31, 37
    content 31, 33
    coverage 26, 29
    definition 20
    functions 21
    indexing 26

negative 22, 35
surveys 54
See also Editing; Reviewers
Riggs, Robert 44
Risk-taking 156-157, 164-165, 168-169, 192-194
Rolling Stone 4
RQ vi, 8, 10-12, 14, 28, 34
Rutgers University 112, 129

*S*aturday Review 4
Scholarly communication 12, 19, 25, 36, 42, 44, 58
See also Informal communication
School Library Journal 33
Schrader, Alvin M. 72, 73, 83, 84, 86, 93
Science Citation Index 4
Sealock, Richard B. 105
Seldin, Peter 142, 148
Service philosophy 15, 43, 60, 64, 65, 178-195
See also Professional commitment; Professional ethics; Professional service
Sessa, Frank B. 118, 119, 125
Sharp, David W. 55
Shaw, Ralph R. 128
Shera, Jesse H. 72, 119
Short, Dorothy 105
Sloan, Elaine F. 120
Smith, Alan Jay 50
Smith, Jessie Carney 119
Smith, Lillian 21
Social Sciences Citation Index x, 4
Software reviews 20
See also CD-ROM database reviews; Databases
Special Libraries Association 98

Index

Sperber, Irwin 62
Staff development 160, 180-186
Stallmann, Esther 78, 80
Stevens, Rolland 105, 118
Stokes, Katharine M. 105, 109
Stokes, Roy 108
Stone, Elizabeth W. 76, 128
Structure of Scientific Revolutions, The 48
Stueart, Robert D. 120
Summers, F. William 6, 74, 78
Sutton, Nancy 105
Swank, Raynard C. 119
Swoboda, Marion J. 170
Sy, Karen 31

*T*almadge, Robert 105, 118
Tauber, Maurice F. 118, 119
Taylor, Francis 105
Tenure **See** Promotion and tenure
Thermodynamics 60 **See also** Maxwell's Demon
Thompson, Lawrence S. 105
Tollefson, Horace A. 118
Tomaino, Mary Y. 117
Torah 3
Trotier, Arnold H. 105
Tuttle, Helen Welch 118, 129

*U*lrich, Carolyn vi
University mission 137
University of Illinois 104, 105, 107, 108, 116
University of Illinois Press 129
University of Minnesota v
University of Pittsburgh v, 116-117, 125-126

University of Southern California 108

Video Annual vi
Von Bertalanffy, Ludwig 53
Vyhnanek, Louis A. 168

Wayne State University 129
Webreck, Susan J. 29
Weedman, Judith 29
Weinstock, Irwin 54
Welch, Helen **See** Tuttle, Helen Welch
West Virginia Libraries v, vi
West Virginia Library Association v
West Virginia University v
Wiegand, Wayne A. 132, 133
Wight, Edward A. 74
Wilson Library Bulletin 8, 30
Wilson, Eugene H. 118
Wilson, Louis Round 78
Winger, Howard W. 105, 119
Wong, Paul T. P. 54
Woods, Bill 118
Woolf, Virginia 22
Woolls, Blanche 118, 120
Work habits 180-186

Yamamoto, Kaoru 171
Yenawine, Wayne S. 105
Yourman, Madeline 105

Zachert, Martha Jane 119
Zey, Michael 159-161, 163, 164
Ziman, John M. 50

ABOUT THE CONTRIBUTORS

Bert R. Boyce has been a Professor of Library and Information Science at Louisiana State University since 1983, where he currently serves as Dean. Dean Boyce holds master's and doctoral degrees in library and information science from Case Western Reserve University. Prior to joining the faculty at LSU, he was Chair of the Department of Information Science of the University of Missouri School of Library and Informational Science. He received the American Society for Information Science Outstanding Information Science Teacher Award in 1989. In 1988, he was awarded the American Library Association Jesse Hauk Shera Award for Research for his paper, coauthored with Danny P. Wallace, "Holdings as a Measure of Journal Value," which was subsequently published in *Library & Information Science Research*. His research interests include the representation of information for retrieval, bibliometrics, and information retrieval models. He has also published in the areas of computer-assisted instruction, filing rules, operations research, and bookmobile operations. He has been a friend and colleague of Charles Patterson for the past decade.

John M. Budd is an associate professor with the School of Library and Information Science of Louisiana State University. He earned the M.L.S. degree from Louisiana State University in 1979. While at LSU, he studied with and was an advisee of Dr. Charles Patterson. After receiving the M.L.S., he worked in academic libraries and attended the University of North Carolina at Chapel Hill, where he was awarded a Ph.D. in library and information science. Prior to joining the faculty at LSU, he was on the faculty of the University of Arizona Graduate Library School. Dr. Budd has published articles on a wide variety of subjects in many journals, including *College & Research Libraries, RQ, Library & Information Science Research,* the *Journal of the American Society for Information Science,* and *Scholarly Publishing.* He has been active in the American Library Association, having chaired committees in the Reference and Adult Services Division and the Library Administration and Management Association. He has taken to heart Dr. Patterson's advice to "publish, participate, and party."

Kathleen de la Peña McCook is a professor of library and information science at Louisiana State University, where she has served as dean of both the School of Library and Information Science and the Graduate School. She has been editor of *RQ* and *Public Libraries,* Associate Editor of *Serials Review,* editor of the "Current Issues in Reference and Adult Services" column for *RQ,* and *Reference Service Review*'s "Landmarks of Reference." She has also served on the editorial boards of *Library Trends, Library Quarterly, Serials Review,* and *Urban Academic Librarian.* Dr. McCook is a prolific author of articles, books, and reports, including *Opportunities in Library and Information Science Careers, Adult Services: An Enduring Focus for Public Libraries,* and *Occupational Entry: Library and Information Science Students' Attitudes, Demographics, and Aspirations.* She holds degrees from the University of Wisconsin, the University of Chicago, Marquette Univer-

About the Contributors

sity, and the University of Illinois at Chicago, and has been on the faculties of the University of Illinois at Urbana-Champaign and the University of Wisconsin.

Joseph J. Mika is Professor and Director of the Library Science Program at Wayne State University. Since he assumed that position in 1986, the Program has seen a one hundred percent increase in full-time faculty and an increase in enrollment of nearly 350 percent. Prior to assuming the Directorship at Wayne State, Dr. Mika was Assistant Dean and Associate Professor at the University of Southern Mississippi. He has also held positions in the libraries of Johnson College (Vermont) and the Ohio State University. He holds master's and doctoral degrees in library and information science from the University of Pittsburgh, where he was a student of Dr. Patterson. Dr. Mika is the author or editor of four monographs and reports and has written more than three dozen articles, reviews, grant proposals, and reports. He is active in the American Library Association, the Michigan Library Association, and the Association for Library and Information Science Education. Dr. Mika served as national president of Beta Phi Mu from 1989 to 1991.

Donald E. Riggs is Dean, University Library, and a professor in the School of Library and Information Studies at the University of Michigan. He has held previous positions at Arizona State University, the University of Colorado at Denver, Metropolitan State College, the Community College of Denver (Auraria Campus), Bluefield State College, and Concord College. He received his M.L.S. from the University of Pittsburgh and an Ed.D. from Virginia Polytechnic Institute and State University. Dr. Riggs is the author of several books, including *Library*

Communication: The Language of Leadership, *Strategic Planning for Library Managers*, and *Libraries in the '90s: What the Leaders Expect*. He studied library and information science under Dr. Charles Patterson at Glenville State College, West Virginia University, and the University of Pittsburgh. "Charles is the one person who initially encouraged me to become a librarian."

Connie Van Fleet is an assistant professor in the Louisiana State University School of Library Science. She holds a bachelor's degree from the University of Oklahoma, a Master of Library and Information Science from Louisiana State University, and a Ph.D. in library and information science from Indiana University. Dr. Van Fleet's publications include articles in *Wilson Library Bulletin*, *Public Libraries*, *The ALA Yearbook of Library and Information Services*, the *Journal of Education for Library and Information Science*, and other periodicals. She has contributed to several books, including two chapters in *Adult Services: An Enduring Focus for Public Libraries*. She is co-editor, with Danny P. Wallace, of *RQ*, the official journal of the Reference and Adult Services Division of the American Library Association. While enrolled in the master's program at LSU, Dr. Van Fleet worked for Dr. Charles Patterson as a graduate research assistant, supporting his work with the *Journal of Education for Library and Information Science* and Beta Phi Mu. "Dr. Patterson was one of my first teachers in library and information science, and I continue to learn from him every day. He has a lot to answer for."

Danny P. Wallace, Associate Dean of the School of Library and Information Science at Louisiana State University, has held faculty positions at the University of Iowa

About the Contributors

and Indiana University and has served as a visiting professor at the University of North Texas. Articles by Dr. Wallace have appeared in the *Journal of the American Society for Information Science*, *Information Processing & Management*, *Library Trends*, *American Libraries*, *Library Journal*, *Law Library Journal* and other library and information science periodicals. Dr. Wallace has served on the ALISE Communications and Public Relations Committee and the ALISE Library and Information Science Education Statistics Project Committee, and is the author of the "Students" section of the 1992 ALISE *Library and Information Science Education Statistical Report*. Dr. Wallace holds a Bachelor of Science in Education from Southwest Missouri State University, a Master of Arts in Library Science from the University of Missouri and a Ph.D. in Library and Information Science from the University of Illinois. "I am very proud to have served on a faculty that included Dr. Charles Patterson; he is a model for the principles of active service and good teaching."

Dana Watson is currently a candidate for the doctoral degree at the University of Alabama School of Library and Information Studies. She received her M.L.I.S. degree at Louisiana State University, where she not only studied under Dr. Charles Patterson, but also served as his graduate assistant, assisting with the editing of the *Journal of Education for Library and Information Science* and with Dr. Patterson's Beta Phi Mu responsibilities. Prior to entering doctoral studies, she served as Consultant, Educational Media Team, Calgary (Alberta) Board of Education, where her responsibilities included coordinating collection development for more than 120 schools. Dr. Patterson's insistence on high professional standards continues to shape her vision. "You can't thank people enough!" reflects Dr.

Patterson's personal interactions with his colleagues. Thank you, Dr. Patterson, for your contributions to me, personally, and to the profession.